THE EXPLORERS AND SETTLERS

A SOURCEBOOK ON COLONIAL AMERICA

THE EXPLORERS AND SETTLERS

A SOURCEBOOK ON COLONIAL AMERICA

Edited by Carter Smith

AMERICAN ALBUMS FROM THE COLLECTIONS OF
THE LIBRARY OF CONGRESS

THE MILLBROOK PRESS, *Brookfield, Connecticut*

Cover: Chart of the East Coast of Virginia, watercolor by John White, 1585-1587.

Title Page: English Settlers at Savanah, engraving, 1773.

Contents Page: Devisal of arms of the Virginia Company of London.

Back Cover: New York harbor from Hobuck Ferry House, hand-colored engraving by Francis Jukes after a drawing by Alexander Robertson, 1800.

Library of Congress Cataloging-in-Publication Data

The Explorers and Settlers: a sourcebook on colonial America / edited by
   Carter Smith.
      p. cm. -- (American albums from the collections of the Library of
   Congress)
      Includes bibliographical references and index.
      Summary: Describes and illustrates the first discoveries and settle-
   ments in North America through a variety of images produced at that
   time.
      ISBN 1-56294-035-X
      1. United States--History--Colonial period, ca. 1600-1775--Juvenile
   literature. 2. United States--History--Colonial period, ca. 1600-1775--
   Pictorial works--Juvenile literature. 3. United States--History--Colonial
   period, ca. 1600-1775--Sources--Juvenile literature. [1. America--
   Discovery and exploration--Sources. 2. United States-History--Colonial
   --period, ca. 1600-1775--Sources.] I. Smith, C. Carter. II. Series.
   E188.E96   1991
   973.2--dc20   91-13939
                                                        CIP
                                                        AC

▇▊ Created in association with Media Projects Incorporated

C. Carter Smith, *Executive Editor*
Lelia Wardwell, *Managing Editor*
Charles A. Wills, *Consulting Editor*
Kimberly Horstman, *Researcher*
Lydia Link, *Designer*
Athena Angelos, *Photo Researcher*

The consultation of Bernard F. Reilly, Jr., Head Curator of the
Prints and Photographs Division of the Library of Congress, is
gratefully acknowledged.

10 9 8 7 6 5 4 3 2 1

Contents

James Edward Oglethorpe (1696-1785), an English general and philanthropist, became a member of Parliament in 1722. His efforts to bring about prison reforms in 1729 gave him the idea to found a colony in North America that would provide a fresh start for the poor. Four years later, he founded Georgia as an asylum for debtors and a haven for persecuted Protestants. He was a popular leader and directed the colony's affairs, particularly its military operations, until his return to England in 1743.

Introduction

THE EXPLORERS AND SETTLERS is one of the volumes in a series published by the Millbrook Press titled AMERICAN ALBUMS FROM THE COLLECTIONS OF THE LIBRARY OF CONGRESS, and one of six books in the series subtitled SOURCEBOOKS ON COLONIAL AMERICA. They treat the early history of our homeland from its discovery and early settlement through the Revolutionary War.

THE EXPLORERS AND SETTLERS reproduces many of the original prints, maps, and book illustrations preserved in the Library of Congress special collections divisions. Most images in this volume come from the extensive holdings of early travel accounts and maps housed in the Library's Rare Book and Special Collections Division, and Geography and Maps Division. The Rare Book Division's John Boyd Thacher and Lessing J. Rosenwald collections are particularly rich in fifteenth, sixteenth, and seventeenth-century illustrated books chronicling the early voyages of exploration and settlement in the New World. The early maps and atlases of the Melville Eastham and other Geography and Map Division collections are also well represented here. A number of the modern views of early buildings, such as the Governor's Palace in Santa Fe, New Mexico, are from the massive documentation of American architecture compiled since the 1930s by the Historic American Buildings Survey, and now preserved in the Library's Prints and Photographs Division. This collection, consisting of measured drawings, photographs, and other pictorial and textual documentation, is the most comprehensive existing record of the historic buildings and building types of the United States.

THE EXPLORERS AND SETTLERS acquaints the student with some of the earliest surviving eyewitness portrayals of the New World. The prints and maps included were part of the great mass of new intelligence about the West Indies which poured into Europe during the era of exploration. Jacques Le Moyne de Morgues's drawings and maps of Florida, reproduced as engravings in Theodore de Bry's *Historia Americae, sive Novi Orbis...*, were based on that artist's own experiences in the French settlement there in 1562. The engravings of the native inhabitants of Virginia encountered by the early British colonists, which appeared in Thomas Hariot's *A Briefe and True Report of the New Found Land of Virginia*, copy the watercolor drawings of John White, an artist sent by Walter Raleigh to help found that British colony.

Other maps and plates appearing here were based upon written accounts rather than first-hand knowledge, such as the imaginative woodcut portrayal of Columbus's discovery of the New World, first published in a 1493 pamphlet. Others, such as Peter Gordon's 1734 plan of the city of Savannah, were produced with ulterior motives—to pay homage to the king of England and to attract speculator interest in the fledgling colony. Many portrayals of the early natives of America are more indicative of European preconceptions of primitive societies than of actual fact.

The documents included here represent a small but telling portion of the rich pictorial record of the American past that the Library of Congress preserves in its role as the national library.

BERNARD F. REILLY, JR.

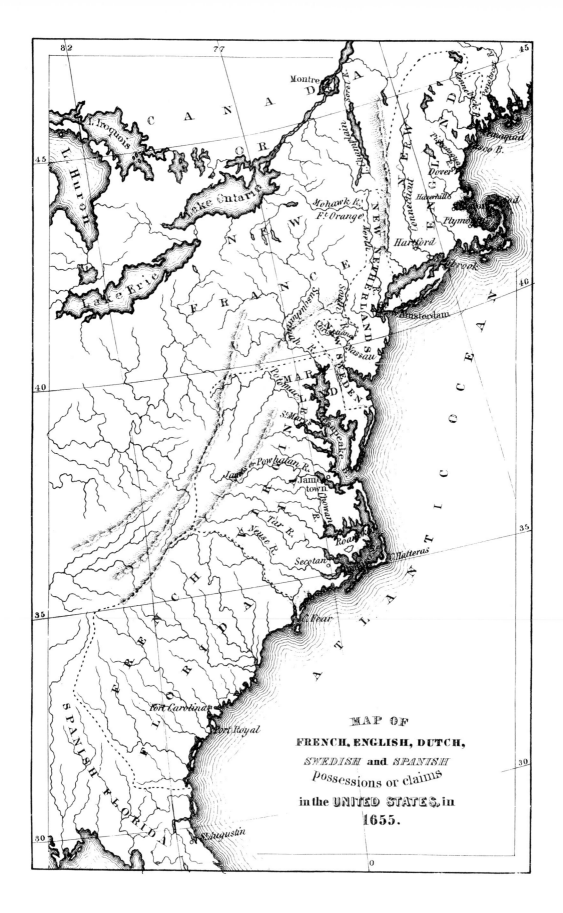

MAP OF
FRENCH, ENGLISH, DUTCH,
SWEDISH and *SPANISH*
Possessions or claims
in the UNITED STATES, in
1655.

The Colonies in 1655

By 1655, the Spanish were well established in the southwest and in Florida; St. Augustine, Spain's first settlement in Florida, was seventy-five years old. France, from a base along the St. Lawrence River, had spread its rich but thinly populated empire of New France south through the valleys of the Mississippi and Ohio rivers. The Dutch had been in New Amsterdam and the Hudson River Valley for a quarter century in 1650; in that time they had also absorbed the small Swedish colony on the Delaware River.

In 1655, English settlement centered in two areas: Chesapeake Bay in the south and Massachusetts Bay in New England. The French and Spanish used rivers as gateways into the interior of the continent, but the English, more by chance than anything else, settled on the coast. From these "beachheads" settlement pushed westward, but in all the English colonies most people lived within a few miles of the seashore.

In the southern colonies of Virginia and Maryland, the tidewater of the Chesapeake Bay provided a means of getting tobacco from plantation to ship for transport to England. In New England, the sea itself was a source of livelihood; by the middle 1600s, the economy of Massachusetts depended so heavily on fishing that a wooden codfish hung in the colony's state house. (It is still there today). The Dutch colony of New Netherland, too, depended on both the river and the sea. The Hudson provided a highway into the fur-rich regions, while New Amsterdam, with its excellent harbor, was on its way to becoming a major port.

Part I: 1490-1599
The First Landings and Explorations

On August 3, 1492, Christopher Columbus set sail from Spain, hoping to chart a new course to Asia. Commanding three small ships—the Santa Maria, *the* Niña, *and the* Pinta— *Columbus sailed due west and then southwest. Two months later, he landed in the New World, probably on Watling's Island in the Bahamas.*

The first Europeans to come to North America were the Vikings, who reached Greenland in about 1000 A.D. European colonization of the New World began with Columbus's first journey, in 1492. Yet the Americas had been colonized thousands of years earlier by Native Americans who had migrated from Asia. These first Americans explored the two continents, establishing both permanent and temporary settlements throughout North and South America. By the 1490s, when European explorers accidentally discovered the continent while seeking new passages to the trading ports of Asia, the first Americans had lived in the "New World" for almost 20,000 years. The riches that Columbus brought back to the Spanish monarchs who had sponsored his journey led to a wave of Spanish explorations in the century that followed.

As the explorers moved north and west from Central America and Florida throughout North America, their mission shifted from exploration and discovery to seizing resources, conquering the Indians, and claiming new territory through colonization. As the sixteenth century went on, France and England sent their own ships to the Americas. Competition for land in the New World led to violent clashes between Spanish and French colonists in the southeast and between Spanish and English explorers in the Caribbean and on the Pacific coast. By the beginning of the seventeenth century, the three major European powers had all staked claims in North America: the Spanish in Florida and the southwest; the French in the northeast; and the English on the mid-Atlantic coast.

A TIMELINE OF MAJOR EVENTS

PART I *1490-1599 The First Landings and Explorations*

WORLD HISTORY

Columbus sets out for America

1492 Spain is finally united under Ferdinand and Isabella; the nation is now able to devote attention to exploration. Christopher Columbus claims North America for Spain.
• Granada, the last Muslim city in Spain, surrenders to Ferdinand and Isabella.

1498 Louis XII becomes king of France on the death of Charles VIII.
• Vasco da Gama of Portugal reaches India.

1510 Portugal founds the first European colony at Goa, in India.

1513 The Portuguese reach Canton, China.

1517 The Protestant Reformation begins: Martin Luther, a Catholic monk in Germany, nails his "Ninety-five Theses" (complaints about failings in the Roman Catholic Church) to the door of the church in Wittenberg.

1519 Charles I of Spain becomes ruler of the Holy Roman Empire, which includes much of Central Europe.

Charles I of Spain

COLONIAL HISTORY

c.**985** Vikings discover and colonize the North Atlantic island of Greenland.

c.**1000** Viking Leif Ericson sails west from Greenland and finds a fertile land he names Vinland; Vinland may have been New England, but recent archaeological discoveries point to eastern Canada as the most probable site.

c.**1015** According to Norse (Viking) sagas, or historical accounts, a Viking colony in Vinland survives for many years.

1492 With Spain's backing, Italian sea captain Christopher Columbus sails from Palos, Spain, with three ships, the *Niña*, the *Pinta*, and the *Santa María*. His aim is to reach the rich lands of Asia by sailing west.
• Columbus makes the first European landfall in the Americas since the Vikings. The site is

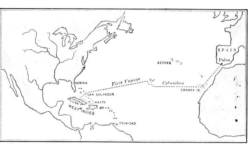

Map of Columbus's voyage to Hispaniola

probably Watling's Island, part of the Bahamas, in the Caribbean Sea.
• Columbus establishes a settlement (which later fails) on an island he calls Hispaniola. He returns to Spain certain he has reached Asia.

1497 Italian-born navigator John Cabot (Giovanni Caboto), now sailing for England's King Henry VII, reaches the island of Newfoundland, off the coast of Canada.

1498 Cabot makes a second voyage to North America in search of the

Northwest Passage.

1507 Italian merchant Amerigo Vespucci claims to have reached the mainland of the New World; his claim is disputed, but the New World becomes known as America (from the Latin form of Amerigo) when German mapmaker Martin Waldseemuller uses the term on a map.

1508 Juan Ponce de León captures the island of Puerto Rico for Spain.

1510 Vasco Núñez de Balboa founds the Spanish settlement of

Darien, on the Atlantic coast of the isthmus of Panama.

1513 Seeking a mythical "fountain of youth," Juan Ponce de León of Spain lands in a part of North America he names Florida.
• After traveling overland from Darien, Balboa becomes the first European to see the Pacific Ocean from its western side.

Hernando Cortés

1519 Spanish explorer Hernando Cortés lands in Mexico; within two years, he and his expedition defeat the rich and powerful Aztec empire and claim Mexico for Spain.

1520 Ferdinand Magellan, a Portuguese explorer and navigator sailing for Spain, reaches the Pacific Ocean by sailing through the straits named after him at the foot of the South American continent. He is killed in the Philippine Islands the next year.
• Suleiman I, "The Magnificent," becomes sultan (ruler) of Turkey; Turkey's empire now includes Arabia.

1521 At the Diet of Worms (a meeting of Catholic prelates in Worms, Germany), Martin Luther is excommunicated from the Catholic Church and is banned from the Holy Roman Empire.

1522 Magellan's successor, Captain Sebastián del Cano, completes the round-the-world trip, returning to Lisbon with one ship out of the original five that began the voyage.

1526 The Mogul dynasty is established in India.

1534 The English Parliament passes the Act of Supremacy acknowledging Henry VIII as head of the Church of England, beginning the English Reformation.

Ferdinand Magellan

1525 Giovanni da Verrazano, an Italian explorer employed by France, reaches the North American coast; sailing north from the Carolinas, he discovers New York Harbor and the Hudson River, named at a later date for explorer Henry Hudson.
• Pedro de Quexco explores a huge bay on the North American coast, later known as Chesapeake Bay.

1527 Spanish explorer Panfilo de Nárvaez lands on the Gulf Coast of North America with 400 explorers. The expedition is a disaster; all but a handful of members die of disease, in Indian attacks, or trying to return to Mexico by sea.
• The English ship *Mary Guilford* sails south along North America's Atlantic coast, from Canada, to Florida.

1533 Francisco Pizarro, a Spanish explorer, conquers the great Inca

Jacques Cartier

empire in South America.

1534 Jacques Cartier of France, lands at the mouth of the St. Lawrence River and claims the surrounding land for France.

1535 Cartier makes a second voyage to North America, this time in search of the wealthy (and mythical) kingdom of Saguenay; he sails down the St. Lawrence as far as modern-day Montreal.
• Antonio de Mendoza arrives in Mexico as the first viceroy (governor) of New Spain, the name given to Spain's empire in the New World.

• The survivors of the Nárvaez expedition, including Cabeza de Vaca, reach Mexico City; they have spent years in Mexico and the Southwest, mostly as prisoners of the Indians.

1539 Franciscan monk Marcos de Niza reports seeing the fabled Cibola (seven cities of gold) while traveling in the Southwest.
• Estevanico, a black former slave and a survivor of the Nárvaez expedition, is killed by Indians while searching

for Cibola with Marcos de Niza.
• Hernando de Soto, along with 600 men, sets out to explore the region that becomes the southwestern United States; he also discovers a survivor of the Nárvaez expedition living with the Indians.
• Several Spanish expeditions claim the California coast for Spain, although no permanent settlements are attempted.

Hernando de Soto

A TIMELINE OF MAJOR EVENTS

PART I *1490-1599 The First Landings and Explorations*

1540 · 1559

WORLD HISTORY

Ignatius Loyola

1541 Ignatius Loyola is elected General of the Society of Jesus (Jesuits), a religious order he founds.

1542 Pope Paul III approves the founding of an Inquisition to combat Protestantism.

1544 The English Parliment officially recognizes Princess Mary (daughter of King Henry VIII and Catherine of Aragon) and Princess

Elizabeth (daughter of Henry and Anne Boleyn) as heirs to the crown in the event that Prince Edward dies without children.

1550 The Spanish bring North America's first beef cattle to Florida.

1555 French astrologer Nostradamus publishes his *Centuries,* a collection of prophesies supposedly foretelling world history and events for the next 500 years.

1556 Akbar becomes Mogul Emperor of India after the death of his father, Humayan. At the battle of Panipat the Moguls defeat the Hindus and secure their empire.

1558 Scottish preacher John Knox publishes his *First Blast of the Trumpet against the Monstrous Regiment of Women,* an attack upon female monarchs.

COLONIAL HISTORY

1540 A large expedition, commanded by Francisco Vásquez de Coronado, leaves Mexico and heads north through the Southwest. The expedition travels through the present-day states of Arizona, Kansas, New Mexico, Oklahoma, and Texas.
• Hernando de Alvarado travels along the Rio Grande into New Mexico.

1541 Jacques Cartier makes his last voyage to North America; he explores the country around the Ottawa River and establishes a settlement at Quebec.

1541 Hernando de Soto's expedition discovers the Mississippi River, near the present site of Memphis, Tennessee.

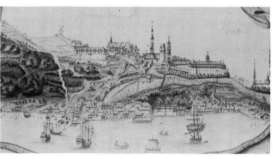

Quebec

Coronado's Expedition

1542 The Coronado expedition returns to Mexico. The journey is considered a failure because Coronado did not find gold, but the explorers discover the Grand Canyon and add a huge region to Spain's empire.
• A Spanish naval expedition under Juan Rodriguez Cabrillo reaches San Diego Bay, California; after Cabrillo's death, Bartelome Ferillo leads the expedition further north along the California coast to San Francisco Bay.

1543 The Hernando de Soto expedition (minus its leader, who dies in 1542) returns to Mexico.

1559 Tristan de Luna y Arellano leads a Spanish expedition to Pensacola, Florida, to establish a settlement; The colony fails and the survivors leave two years later.

1560 A meeting of the Scottish parliament abolishes the Pope's authority in Scotland.

1561 John Knox publishes his *Book of Discipline,* outlining a Calvinistic constitution for the Scottish church.

1563 The "Thirty-nine Articles" of the Church of England are published.
• A plague sweeps London, killing more than 17,000 people.

1564 Michelangelo, the great Italian painter, sculptor, and architect, dies.

1570 The Portuguese begin trading with Japan at Nagasaki.

1577 Francis Drake sails from Portsmouth, England, for the Pacific coast of South America, where he intends to harass Spanish shipping. His voyage eventually takes him around the world.

Sir Francis Drake

1562 Jean Ribaut of France leads 150 settlers to the coast of what is now South Carolina, in an attempt to found a refuge for French Protestants (Huguenots); the colony is abandoned soon after.

1564 A second French colonizing expedition, commanded by René de Laudonnière, lands in what is today Florida.

1565 Alarmed at the French presence close to Spanish Florida, a force under Pedro Menéndez de Avilés, attacks the colony, destroying it and killing almost all the settlers.
• Spain establishes St. Augustine, its chief outpost in Florida and the oldest permanent European settlement in what is now the United States.

1571 Spanish attempts to colonize northern Florida (now part of Virginia) fail when Indians overrun a

Jesuit mission on the southern portion of the Chesapeake Bay.

1576 Queen Elizabeth I grants Sir Humphrey Gilbert a patent (royal authority) to colonize the New World for England and the crown.

1579 English captain Francis Drake's round-the-world expedition reaches San Francisco Bay, California; he claims the area for England, naming it New Albion. (Albion is another name for England.)

1583 Sir Humphrey Gilbert founds a colony on the island of Newfoundland off the coast of Canada. Gilbert is lost at sea while returning to England and his patent passes to his half brother, Walter Raleigh.

1584 Captains Philip Amadas and Arthur Barlowe, sailing for Walter Raleigh, sail to the New World to pave

A Roanoke chief

the way for an English colony in the Chesapeake Bay region.

1585 Raleigh names the land explored by his expedition "Virginia," in honor of England's unmarried queen.
• More than one hundred colonists under Governor Richard Grenville establish a colony in Virginia, on Roanoke Island off the coast of modern-day North Carolina.

1586 The first Roanoke colony fails; those colonists who survive are taken back to England by Sir Francis Drake, who arrives at Roanoke after burning the Spanish fort at St. Augustine. Not realizing the colony had been abandoned, a relief expedition commanded by Sir Richard Grenville sails to Roanoke; Grenville leaves about fifteen men on Roanoke and returns to England.

1587 Another colonizing expedition arrives at Roanoke, bringing more than one hundred settlers led by John White. The expedition finds only the bones of the settlers left by Grenville in 1586; White sails back to England for more supplies.
• Virginia Dare is born to Ananias and Eleanor Dare of the Roanoke Colony; she is the first child born of English parents in North America.

THE EARLIEST SETTLERS

Long before Europeans set foot in North America, people had settled on the continent. They began migrating from Asia to North America perhaps as early as 20,000 years ago. These migrants probably crossed over to North America at or near the Bering Strait, which separates Alaska and Asia by only fifty-three miles. They may have come by sea or by a temporary bridge of land formed when the water level of the sea dropped. The early North Americans migrated eastward and then southward, spreading throughout the continent over thousands of years. The migrating peoples gradually adapted to their new homes and developed different cultures. Some communities subsisted by hunting, fishing, gathering wild plants, farming, or some combination of these practices. The people from Asia became the first settlers of North America, forming either permanent or seasonal villages and living off the rich land and its abundant resources.

Over two thousand years ago, ancient Indian cultures, especially those who had permanent villages, often built burial mounds to honor their dead. Burial mounds housed the bodies of the dead as well as offerings made by the people to ensure their peace after death. These mounds varied widely in shape, size, and decoration, according to tribal custom. The Hopewell Mound, or the Great Serpent Mound (opposite page, top), in Adams County, Ohio, stands five feet tall and stretches for 1,254 feet. It seems to depict a snake with an egg in its mouth.

In the southwest region of North America, some Indian cultures established magnificent dwellings in recesses on the faces of cliffs, as shown in this nineteenth-century sketch (opposite page, bottom). The Anasazi (Navajo for the "Ancient Ones") began building cliff houses of log, adobe (dried mud bricks), and stone in the eleventh or twelfth century. These cliff dwellings, which housed entire tribes, stood as high as five stories and had as many as a thousand rooms. The Anasazi left their cliff houses near the end of the thirteenth century, perhaps because of attacks by the Navajo or Apache tribes or as a result of a long drought.

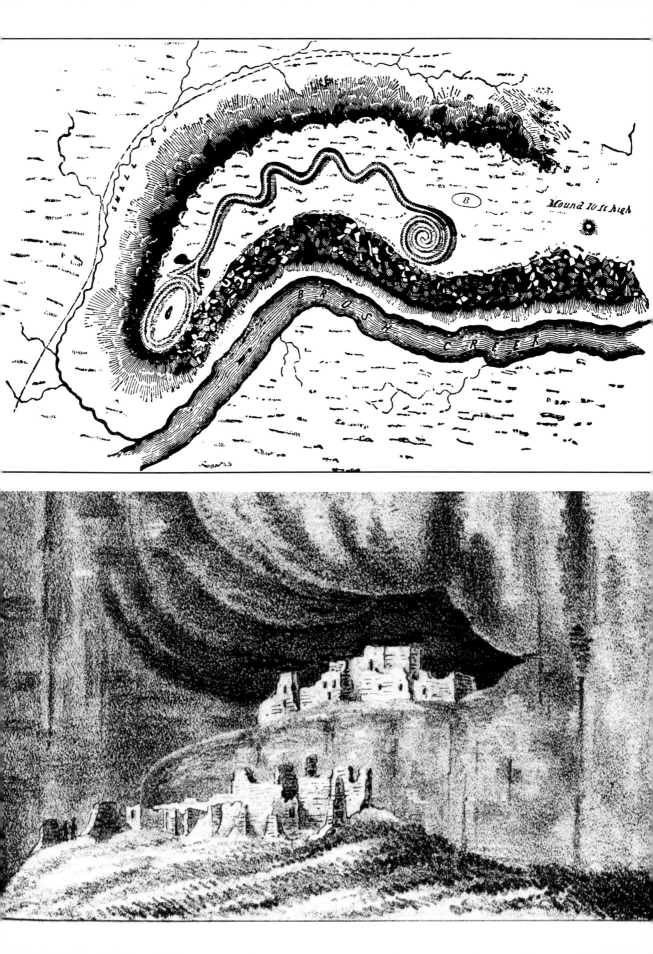

EUROPEAN VIEWS
OF A NEW WORLD

Until the sixteenth century, few Europeans believed in the existence of an unknown continent to the west of their shores. Geographers of the time thought of Europe, Asia, and Africa as the only continents on earth. Fifteenth-century scholars revived the ancient Greek theory that the Earth was round, leading some people to believe that by sailing westward a ship would eventually arrive in Asia. These theories, combined with advances in shipbuilding and better navigational instruments for sailing, made exploration seem possible. The impulse to explore faraway lands was also fueled by the ambitions of both merchants and monarchs. Merchants, always eager to expand trade, became increasingly willing to finance risky ventures that might open up new trading markets. The spice trade with the Orient had become especially important and profitable. Explorers were further encouraged by monarchs who hoped not only to increase trade, but also to gain treasures or new territory.

In 1484, Christopher Columbus first proposed to sail west in hopes of opening up new trade routes to the East. Eight years later, he finally found a receptive audience in Queen Isabella and King Ferdinand of Spain, who decided to sponsor his voyage.

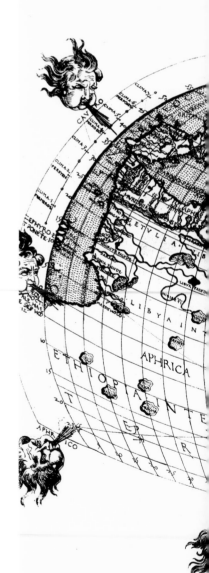

King Ferdinand II (1452-1516) and Queen Isabella I (1451-1504), pictured together in this woodcut (left), jointly ruled Spain from the time of their marriage in 1469 until the queen's death thirty-five years later. In 1492, the Spanish monarchs sponsored the first Atlantic voyage of Christopher Columbus. After conquering the Kingdom of Granada in January 1492, Ferdinand and Isabella decided to back Columbus's quest for a new westward trade route to the rich Indies, as Asia was called at the time. They approved the expedition, which set out in August 1492.

In seeking support for his voyage, Christopher Columbus relied on the ancient map of the world developed in the second century by Ptolemy (below). Ptolemy, a Greek astronomer, mathematician, and geographer, introduced a map that portrayed the earth as round. This incomplete map strengthened Columbus's belief that he could reach Asia directly by sailing westward from Europe.

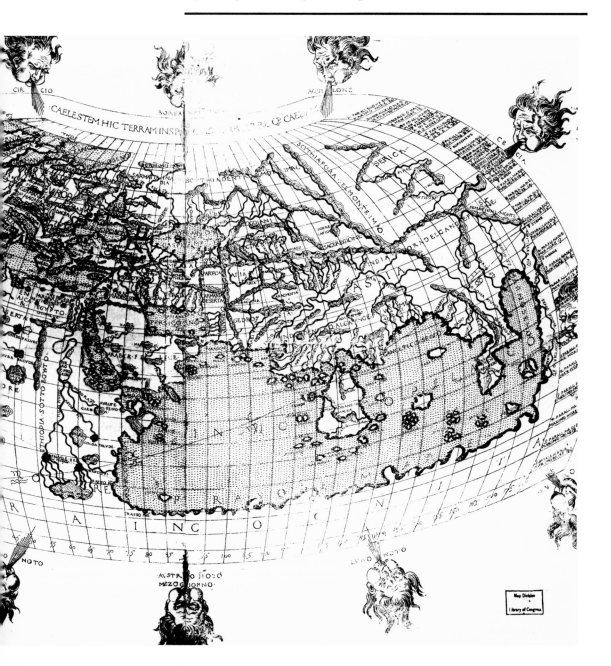

THE VOYAGE OF CHRISTOPHER COLUMBUS

Christopher Columbus (1451-1506), born in Genoa, Italy, first went to sea in his teens. He gained sailing experience in the 1480s while living in the Madeira Islands, off the coast of Portugal. Columbus became convinced that the world was round and that he could sail west and arrive in the East. Through elaborate calculations based upon Ptolemy's map, Columbus estimated that "India" would be west of the Canary Islands (roughly where he found America).

In 1484, he first proposed such a voyage to the King of Portugal, who turned him down. Columbus then approached King Ferdinand and Queen Isabella of Spain. A commission studied the proposal for four years and rejected it at first, but ultimately the king and queen decided to provide funds to send Columbus on the voyage.

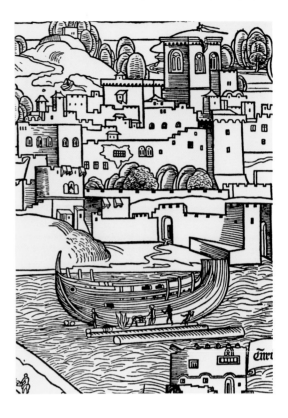

Fifteenth-century improvements in ship design led to the development of the caravel (above). Caravels like the Niña *and the* Pinta *were light vessels, rigged so that they could keep their course even when the wind was blowing in another direction. This ability proved helpful in long sea voyages.*

Improvements in navigational instruments aided Columbus in his journey. The jackstaff (also called the cross-staff or Jacob's staff; pictured left) was used to determine the altitude of certain stars that sailors used as navigational guides. It allowed sailors to determine their own location based on the "shifting" of the stars in relation to the horizon.

Christopher Columbus set sail from Palos, Spain (right), with three small ships—the Santa Maria *(his flagship), and two caravels, the* Niña *and the* Pinta—*on August 3, 1492. From September 9, when the Canary Islands disappeared from sight, until October 12, the crews of the three ships saw no land—only ocean and mirages. For this reason, the ten-week voyage tested Columbus's faith and leadership as much as his navigational skills.*

CHRISTOPHER COLUMBUS DISCOVERS THE NEW WORLD

On October 12, 1492, Christopher Columbus landed on the shore of one of the Bahama Islands. Columbus claimed possession of the land in the name of Ferdinand and Isabella, renaming it San Salvador. Hoping he would soon arrive in Japan, he then moved on to Cuba, describing the island's beauty in glowing terms. "Its lands are lofty and in it there are many high sierras and high mountains. . . . All are most beautiful . . . filled with trees of a thousand kinds, some of them . . . flowering, some with fruit. . . . And there were singing the nightingale and other little birds of a thousand kinds in the month of November."

Columbus soon met the native people of the islands, which he mistakenly called "Indians," thinking he reached the Indies. In a letter widely published throughout Europe in 1493, he wrote, "I have not found the human monstrosities which many people expected." Columbus praised the intelligence, industry, and honor of the natives, yet he saw them chiefly for their potential as forced laborers. He ordered his crew to treat the Indians well in the hope that good treatment would encourage them to convert to Christianity, to trade with the Europeans, and, even more important, to help the Europeans find gold and other New World riches.

Upon his landing, in October 1492, Columbus regarded the natives as fearful and timid. Many ran from the Europeans (above), leaving behind everything they had. He noted the Indians' peacefulness, observing that they carried no weapons. Once the Indians overcame their fear of the strangers they began bartering with Columbus and his crew.

Columbus was impressed with the traditional Indian method of navigating waterways (right). He remarked upon the utility, the beauty and the swiftness of the Indian canoes. The Indians carved canoes, which they used to travel from island to island. Columbus compared the largest of the canoes, which could hold as many as 150 people, with his own ships.

Everything the Europeans owned seemed new and interesting to the Indians. As a result, they traded gold, cotton, and other commodities valued by the Europeans for what Columbus described as "trifles and articles of no value" (such as pieces of glass, keys, and leather straps). To correct the injustice of some greedy crew members, Columbus gave many gifts to the Indians. Columbus's four voyages between 1492 and 1504 yielded great riches. He returned to Spain with gold, spices, parrots, plants, and, sadly, natives to be sold in Europe as slaves.

The Taíno Indians that Columbus first encountered made an unleavened bread from cassava, or yuca root (below). Although the Indians offered this bread to the Europeans, the explorers found the bread practically inedible.

The Taíno Indians lived in communities of huts made of tree branches with palm-thatched roofs. Columbus found that the members of these communities had little notion of private property. He was particularly impressed with the hammocks the Indians slept in (opposite, top), which they made by weaving crossed threads of cotton. Columbus's sailors took several hammocks with them, hanging them on board during their return voyage to Spain.

Columbus heard tales of tribes of Indians that roamed through the islands, capturing and eating all the people they could find. These people were called "Caribs" by the Europeans, and "Caniba" by natives (and eventually cannibals by the English). In time, Columbus encountered these Caribs himself: "people who are regarded in all the islands as very ferocious and who eat human flesh; they have canoes with which they range all the islands of India [sic] and pillage and take as much as they can." This picture (opposite, bottom), one of the earliest representations of New World people, shows a body hanging in smoke to be cured.

SPAIN LAUNCHES MORE EXPLORATIONS

When Columbus returned to Spain, his ship laden with treasures, his success prompted the Spanish monarchs to send more ships to the New World. Columbus himself led three more voyages. His second continued his exploration of the islands of the Caribbean. In fact, he did not set foot on the mainland of the New World, in what is now Venezuela, until his third voyage in 1498.

Columbus died in 1512 believing the lands he had reached were part of Asia, but by then merchants, scholars, and monarchs were realizing that a "New World" had actually been discovered. Armed with this knowledge, the object of Spanish expeditions shifted away from discovery and charting a new course to the Indies, and moved toward capturing new territory and treasure for Spain. Within twenty-five years of Columbus's first landing in the New World, Spanish explorers had claimed lands in North America, Central America, and South America.

Although the truthfulness of his claim is seriously doubted by historians, Amerigo Vespucci (1454-1512) maintained that he discovered mainland America in 1497, one year before Columbus landed briefly in South America. While working with a man who outfitted ships in Seville, Spain, Vespucci, an Italian merchant, helped prepare ships for Columbus's second and third expeditions to the New World. On Vespucci's first documented voyage to the New World (1499-1500), sponsored by Spain, he discovered the mouth of the Amazon River. But his second voyage, supported by Portugal, was more important because it suggested strongly that the New World was not part of Asia.

Most historians feel Vespucci's skill at self-promotion exceeded his abilities as a navigator. Vespucci's claim to have landed in the New World as early as 1497 (above) is dismissed by most historians. Still, his second documented voyage (1501-1502) did convince Vespucci and scholars that the New World was a land separate from Asia. For this reason, the new continents—North and South America—derive their names from his. In 1507, mapmaker Martin Waldseemuller published the first map showing the New World separate from Asia. Waldseemuller named the land America, after Vespucci's first name.

Juan Ponce de León (1460-1521; right), a Spanish explorer, founded a Spanish settlement in Puerto Rico in 1508, and later discovered Florida. Searching for gold, Ponce de León explored Puerto Rico from 1508 to 1509. After a brief term as governor of this island, he set out in search of the legendary "Fountain of Youth," which according to Indian myth restored youth to anyone who drank from it. In his quest for the fountain, Ponce de León came upon a new land in 1513. In 1514, Spain granted him permission to colonize this land, which he named Florida.

HERNANDO DE SOTO

One of the most prominent of all Spanish explorers and conquerors of the Americas was Hernando de Soto (c. 1500-1542), who helped conquer Central America and Peru and later became the first European to discover the Mississippi River. Fascinated by the tales of adventure in the New World that had excited all of Spain, De Soto, when still in his teens, headed for the Spanish provinces on the Caribbean coast. In the 1520s and 1530s, De Soto participated in the conquest of the Incas in Central America and in Peru, gaining a huge personal fortune.

In 1533, Francisco Pizarro, com-mander of the Peruvian expedition, executed the Inca king Atahualpa, whom De Soto had befriended. Apparently disgusted with the brutali-ty of colonial conquest, De Soto returned to Spain in 1536. Just three years later, however, De Soto decided to use his fortune to search for greater treasure. He landed in Florida in 1539 and began exploring the southeastern part of North America. After spending the winter exploring Florida, De Soto headed north and then west in the spring of 1540. On May 21, 1540, his expedition became the first Europeans to sight the mighty river that the Indians called the Mississippi, "Father of the Waters."

Hernando de Soto, unlike many of the other Spanish conquistadores, didn't necessarily set out to conquer the Indians in order to obtain riches. Some Indian tribes welcomed De Soto's presence in their territory, and he apparently negotiated treaties when he could. But De Soto also had several violent encounters with the Native Americans.

This 1718 map of the Louisiana Territory (right) indicates the course of De Soto's expedition to the Mississippi River in 1540. (Titles and descriptions on the map are in French, because by 1718 France had claimed the Louisiana Territory as its own.) De Soto began his exploration in Florida, moving northward into present-day Georgia and the Carolinas. He continued westward through the land that would later become northern Alabama and Tennessee, where he first sighted the Mississippi River. Finally, he crossed into present-day Arkansas and Oklahoma before circling back to the Mississippi River.

The First Landings and Explorations **29**

EXPLORATIONS INLAND AND TO THE WEST

Throughout the sixteenth and seventeenth centuries, Spanish exploration of the New World moved northward and westward across the Americas. Native American legends that told of "cities of gold" or other fantastic treasures inspired some Spanish explorers to venture farther and farther inland. Starting in Central America, Mexico, and Florida, the Spaniards traveled north and west through the North American continent. Although they encountered—and often conquered—many Indian civilizations, the explorers never found the marvelous riches they hoped to find. The Spanish *conquistadores* often treated the Indians they encountered brutally, regarding them as rivals for the riches and resources of the New World.

Spanish explorations of the New World essentially ended with the surveying of the Pacific coastline, to the northernmost border of present-day California in 1542-43. The Spaniards continued to establish colonies, especially in the southwest region of the continent, most notably in what is now New Mexico, at the very end of the century. The settlement established by the Spanish in Santa Fe is the oldest North American city to have served continuously as a seat of government.

Setting out from Mexico City in February 1540, General Francisco Vàsquez de Coronado marched north into the interior of North America (right). Coronado, leading an expedition of three hundred soldiers and missionaries and more than a thousand Indians, hoped to find the legendary "Seven Golden Cities" called Cibola. In July 1540, Coronado arrived at the supposed location of the golden cities, but found nothing more than a poor village of Zuñi Indians.

The city of Santa Fe was founded in 1610 by Spanish settlers under governor Don Pedro de Peralta, making it the oldest existing U.S. capital. Peralta built the governor's palace in the same year. This structure (below), built of adobe, was restored as a museum in 1914.

FRENCH EXPLORATIONS

While Spanish explorers in the sixteenth century concentrated on the southern and western regions of North America, France sent several expeditions to the northeast. However, France was embroiled in a series of wars with Italy that lasted from 1494 until 1559. As a result, the royal government of France was too burdened by military and political struggles at home to sponsor expeditions on the same scale as the Spanish. The first to come bearing the French flag was an Italian, Giovanni da Verrazano, who first reached North America in 1523, in hope that he would discover a westward passage to Asia. Although he was unsuccessful in his quest, Verrazano became the first European to sight New York Harbor and Narragansett Bay.

From 1534 to 1542, the French crown financed three more expeditions to the New World, all led by Jacques Cartier. Again, the expeditions sought both to discover a northwest passage to the Pacific and to acquire New World treasures: gold, spices, and other natural resources. Cartier's failure to achieve these goals discouraged the French monarchs from any further exploration of northeastern North America for over fifty years. Still, his explorations of the St. Lawrence River and North American coast laid the basis for later French claims to the territory that became Canada.

Jacques Cartier (1491-1557; above) undertook his first voyage to the New World in 1534. A year later, with the help of two Indian guides, he discovered the mouth of the St. Lawrence River and sailed all the way to modern-day Quebec. There he endured a brutal winter that killed twenty-five of his crew. His cruel treatment of the Indians, who had at first welcomed the newcomers, aroused hostilities that increased with his third voyage in 1541-1542. Later clashes with the Indians, combined with the harsh winter climate, led to the failure of this attempt at colonization.

Giovanni da Verrazano (c. 1485-1528) went on three expeditions to the Americas. On the first, seeking a northwest passage to the Pacific, Verrazano explored the Atlantic coastline of North America north from the modern Carolinas all the way to Newfoundland. His second voyage took him to Brazil, and his third voyage involved exploration of Florida, and the islands of the Caribbean. Verrazano's map of the New World, shown in part here (right), charts the Atlantic coastline of North and South America.

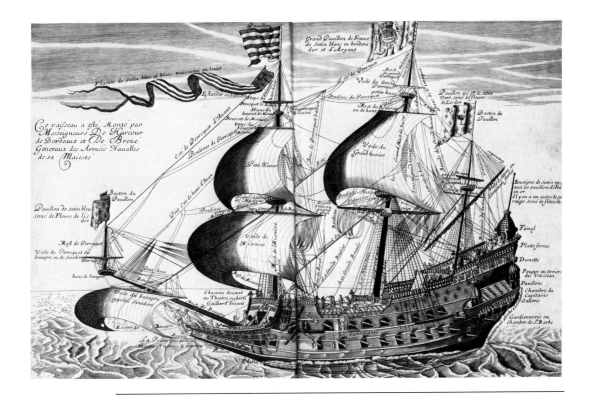

Fifteenth-century European shipbuilders introduced ship design that made over-sea voyages easier. The type of three-masted vessel shown here divided the area of the square sails on the fore and main masts into two or three smaller sails. The old-fashioned ships, with only one mast and sail, soon gave way to these new ships.

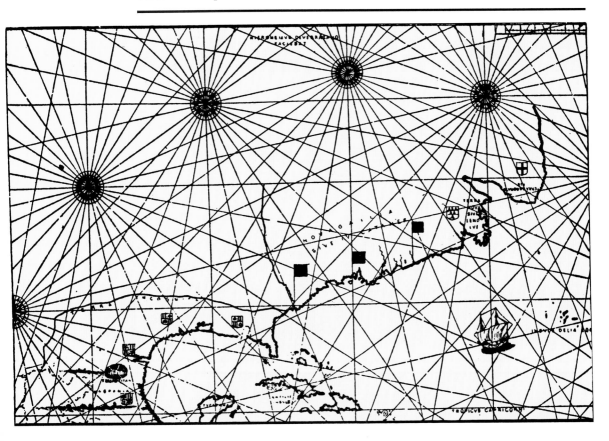

THE FRENCH HUGUENOTS IN FLORIDA

Florida would become an important territory in the struggles of the European powers—Spain, France, and England—to establish dominance in the New World. This struggle began with the arrival of French Huguenots in Florida in 1564. The Huguenots were French Protestants who suffered severe persecution for their faith in mostly Roman Catholic France. Many French Huguenots had been imprisoned or killed in the middle of the sixteenth century. Seeking a place in which to live and worship freely, the Huguenots made several attempts in the 1560s to settle in Florida, where the Spanish had already established settlements.

Lack of food and other supplies drove the first Huguenot colonizing expedition back to France in 1564. A second attempt in 1565 failed because of mutiny and fighting with local Indians. That same year, the French settlement, Fort Caroline, was destroyed by the Spanish. Also in 1565, near the site of this devastated fort, the Spanish founded St. Augustine, the oldest continuously-inhabited city in the United States.

The Huguenots arrived in the New World on June 22, 1564, landing on the Atlantic coast of northern Florida (opposite, top). The new settlers were greeted warmly by the local Indians, who offered the French commander, René de Laudonnière, garments made of skins and "a large skin decorated with pictures of wild animals." The French then explored several rivers along the Atlantic coast of modern-day Florida before deciding to settle along the St. Johns River.

Laudonnière and the Huguenots established the first French settlement in Florida in 1564 near the mouth of the St. Johns River (opposite, bottom). The area was chosen not only for the rich resources of gold and silver in the region, but also for the abundance of food. In 1565, Fort Caroline was wiped out by a force of Spanish colonists, angered by the French presence in Florida. After killing virtually all of the French colonists, the Spanish renamed the fort San Mateo.

F. Dolfinum.

F. Maii

The Florida Indians established semi-permanent villages (above) where they lived throughout the spring, summer, and fall. In these villages, the Indians survived mostly through farming. During the winter, the Indians sought shelter from the cold in the nearby woods. This engraving is based on a painting by Jacques Le Moyne de Morgues, an artist and mapmaker who accompanied one of the French expeditions.

The Florida Indians planted corn and beans in the fall for harvesting the next year (opposite, top). First, the men would till the soil using hoes made from fish bones attached to wooden handles. After they had leveled and broken up the ground, the women would plant the seeds. Some women would make holes for the seeds by plunging sticks into the earth. Others would follow, dropping seeds into the holes.

The native people hunted—and defended themselves against—the fierce alligators that often threatened them (opposite, bottom). When an alligator was sighted, "They take with them a ten-foot pointed pole," Le Moyne wrote, "and when they come upon the monster—who usually crawls along with open mouth, ready to attack—they push the pole quickly down its throat. . . . Then the beast is turned over on its back and killed by beating it with clubs and piercing its soft belly with arrows."

SIR FRANCIS DRAKE

Sir Francis Drake (c. 1540-1596) sailed the first English ship around the world. In 1572, England's Queen Elizabeth I commissioned Drake to plunder Spanish shipping in the New World. Drake won both fame and fortune in a series of daring attacks on Spanish colonies in Panama In 1577, the Queen again chose Drake to lead an expedition around the world—and to disrupt Spanish trade on the Pacific coast of the Americas.

A year later, Drake's ship, the *Golden Hind*, became the first English ship to sail around South America and into the Pacific. While sailing north along the coast, Drake looted unprepared Spanish ships and settlements on the Pacific coast of South America, capturing gold, silver, pearls, and precious stones. Searching for a passage from the Pacific to the Atlantic, Drake explored the northern Pacific Coast in 1579, becoming the first European to sight the west coast of modern-day Canada and later, San Francisco Bay. Drake continued his voyage across the Pacific and Indian oceans, and then sailed home north through the Atlantic.

In command of a twenty-five-ship fleet in 1585, Drake attacked several Spanish cities in the Americas, including Santo Domingo on Hispaniola and Fort Augustine in Florida. After returning to England, Drake scored military victories against the Spanish and helped defeat the mighty armada Spain sent to invade England in 1588.

Upon reaching San Francisco Bay in 1579, Drake and the crew of the Golden Hind *were greeted by friendly Indians from a nearby village (top right). Crewmen who dared to go inland returned with reports of enormous herds of deer. Drake remained in the bay for a month, refitting his ship and resting his crew, who had been at sea for eighteen months. The* Golden Hind *then set sail west to Asia to complete Drake's circumnavigation of the globe.*

Commissioned by the Queen of England to damage Spain's overseas empire, Drake's fleet of twenty-five ships burned St. Augustine, Florida, on June 7, 1586 (bottom right). Drake, known and feared as "El Draque" ("the Dragon") among the Spanish, had already plundered dozens of Spanish cities and settlements before arriving at St. Augustine. The destruction of the city ended Drake's harassment of Spanish holdings in the New World.

THE ENGLISH COLONY AT ROANOKE

By the end of the sixteenth century, England wanted to join Spain and France in gaining a foothold in the New World. Sir Walter Raleigh organized the first attempts by the English to colonize the New World at Roanoke Island (off the coast of modern-day North Carolina) in the 1580s. Roanoke was first explored in 1584 by captains Philip Amadas and Arthur Barlowe. The first English colonists settled the island in 1585 and quickly established trade with the local Indians. According to Barlowe, the Native Americans received them "with all love and kindness, and with as much bounty, after their manner, as they could possibly devise." The colony failed in June 1586, when the colonists, discouraged by the lack of supplies and the threat of Indian hostilities, abandoned Roanoke and returned to England.

A second attempt to colonize Roanoke, in 1587, became known as the "Lost Colony." Governor John White's supply ships, delayed by the Spanish Armada, failed to return to Roanoke until August 1590. By then, all of the colonists had disappeared, leaving no clue to their fate except the word "Croatoan"—the name of a nearby Indian tribe—carved into a tree. Shaken by the mysterious disappearance of the Lost Colony, the English didn't return to the area for almost twenty years.

Sir Walter Raleigh (c. 1554-1618), an English adventurer, writer, and favorite of Queen Elizabeth I, was knighted in 1585, partly in recognition of his effort to extend British rule to the New World. Although Raleigh didn't visit the New World until ten years after the first attempt to colonize Roanoke Island, he deserves credit for organizing the expedition. Raleigh later led a 1595 expedition to South America, at the site of present-day Guyana. Although he supported colonization there, he failed to win enough support to make this venture possible. After falling out of favor with the English government, Raleigh was executed in 1618.

Thomas Hariot, a mathematician and astronomer, served as Raleigh's scientific adviser for the first expedition to Roanoke Island. After his return from the failed colony, Hariot published his observations in A Briefe and True Report of the New Found Land of Virginia *(right)*. This volume—illustrated by John White, who would become governor of the second expedition to Roanoke—described the land and its native inhabitants. This report, first published in 1588, was widely reprinted in the following years.

Three months after leaving England, the *Tiger* and the *Dorothy* landed on the coast of present-day North Carolina on July 4, 1584 *(below)*. The two ships, captained by Philip Amadas and Arthur Barlowe, had stopped briefly in Puerto Rico and Florida before heading north along the Atlantic coast. Upon landing in North Carolina, the explorers boldly claimed the entire Atlantic coastline for England and named it Virginia, after the "virgin queen," Elizabeth I of England.

THE
VIRGINIA INDIANS

Though sixteenth-century English attempts to colonize the New World failed, Raleigh's explorers brought back extensive reports of the people and places they encountered. John White's watercolors and sketches, used to illustrate Thomas Hariot's *A Brief and True Report* and later translated into engravings by Theodore de Bry, were especially informative. White, a member of the first colonization expedition, served as governor of the second colony at Roanoke. (White's granddaughter, Virginia Dare, was the first English child born in the New World.) His paintings and sketches of the land, people, animals, and plants of the New World provided the people of England with their first view of the native population of North America.

Indian towns consisted of a cluster of houses surrounded by fields and forests. As painted by John White in 1586, this portrayal of Secota (above), a small Indian village, shows tobacco, corn, and pumpkins growing in the gardens behind the village houses. The Indians hunted deer in the nearby woods (upper left corner). "These people live happily together without envy or greed," White reported. Villagers gathered together every night for prayer, feasts, and celebrations.

The Virginia Indians ate from a mat laid on the ground (below). Everyone would sit around the mat—the men on one side and the women on the other. The diet of Virginia Indians consisted of fish, deer, and other meat, accompanied by corn, squash, and other vegetables previously unknown to Europeans.

The Virginia Indians caught fish using spears and traps. The Indians constructed spears by attaching sharp fish bones to reeds or long rods. Reeds or sticks were interwoven to form fish traps, as shown at the back of the canoe (above). The English colonists reported an abundance of fish, of many varieties and "excellent taste."

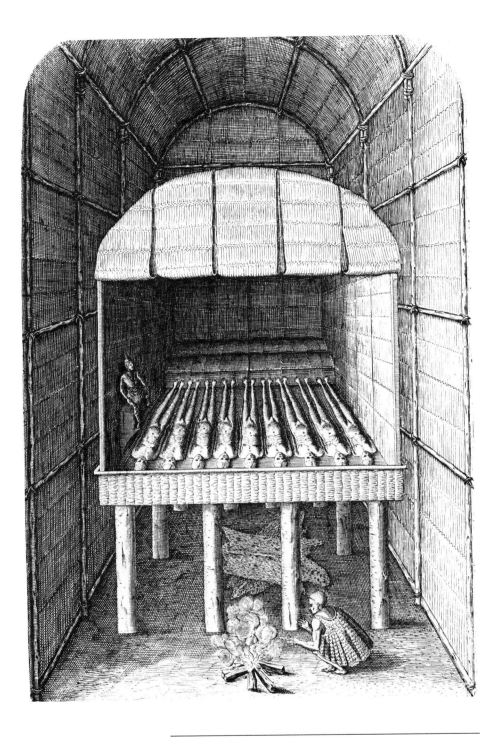

Every town had a large building that housed the tombs
of the village leaders. When chiefs died, their skins
were removed from their skeletons, dried, and then
used to cover their bones. Each corpse was then laid
upon a nine- or ten-foot platform, next to the bodies of
previous chiefs (above). A caretaker lived in the tombs,
praying night and day for the dead leaders.

THE PORTRAICTUER OF CAPTAYNE IOHN SMITH ADMIRALL OF NEW ENGLAND.

Ætia 37.
Aᵒ 1616

Part II: 1600-1649
In Search of New Lands:
The Quest for Freedom and Prosperity

English adventurer and soldier Captain John Smith (1580-1631) was one of the most important members of the 1607 expedition that established Jamestown. In 1608, Smith took over the leadership of the failing colony, and his policy of firm discipline and hard work helped the colonists survive the winter of 1608-1609.

By the beginning of the seventeenth century, Spain had established itself as the major power in the New World. The first half of the century brought new colonization attempts by France and England, as well as smaller efforts by the Dutch. The French became the dominant European settlers in what would become the nation of Canada. Quebec, the first permanent French settlement in the New World, became the capital of France's North American empire and the center of the growing French fur trade.

The English founded permanent colonies in Virginia and New England. The Jamestown colony, founded in 1607, survived its difficult first years to become a center for tobacco production. The Plymouth and Massachusetts Bay colonies were both founded by settlers seeking a land where they could freely practice their own religions. Some English settlers, seeking even greater freedom, left to found new colonies in Connecticut and Rhode Island. Dutch settlers, following the expedition Henry Hudson led up the Hudson River in 1609, established a number of settlements on the Hudson and Delaware rivers, led by the thriving commercial center of New Amsterdam on Manhattan Island. At first, life was a struggle for all the European colonists: Three-quarters of Quebec's colonists, two-thirds of Jamestown's colonists, and one-half of the Plymouth colonists died less than a year after landing in North America. The survivors, however, established a firm European foothold in the New World.

A TIMELINE OF MAJOR EVENTS

PART II *1600-1649 In Search of New Lands: The Quest for Freedom and Prosperity*

1 6 0 0 · 1 6 1 6

WORLD HISTORY

Queen Elizabeth I

1600 Queen Elizabeth I of England grants a charter to the East India Company, permitting it to trade in the East Indies for the next fifteen years.

1602 The Dutch East India Company is incorporated in Holland.

1603 Queen Elizabeth I of England dies. She is succeeded by James VI, who unites the thrones of England and Scotland, and rules as James I.

1605 Spanish author Miguel de Cervantes publishes part I of his novel *Don Quixote de la Mancha*.
• The Golden Temple at Amritsar, the main shrine of the Sikh religion, is completed.
• The Mogul emperor Akbar the Great dies at Agra, India.
• William Shakespeare's tragedy *Macbeth* is performed for the first time in London.

1611 A new English translation of the Bible, authorized by King James, is published.

1615 An English fleet defeats the Portuguese off Bombay.

1616 Poet and playwright William Shakespeare, greatest writer of the Elizabethan era and probably in all English literature, dies at his home in Stratford-upon-Avon.

COLONIAL HISTORY

1602 After exploring and naming Cape Cod and Martha's Vineyard, Bartholomew Gosnold returns from America to England with a cargo of furs and lumber, fueling the movement to colonize North America.
• Sebastian Vizcaíno explores a bay on the coast of central California and names it Monterey after the Count of Monte Rey, viceroy of Mexico.

1603 Samuel de Champlain embarks on the first of eleven exploratory voyages along the St. Lawrence River and the northeastern Atlantic coast of North America.

1604 Champlain and Pierre de Monts establish the first French settlement in Acadia on an island in Passamaquoddy Bay, along the present-day United States-Canada border.

1606 The London and Plymouth companies receive charters from King James I of England to establish colonies in the New World.

John Smith

1607 Under the charter granted to the Virginia Company of London, an expedition led by Bartholomew Gosnold, John Smith, and Christopher Newport founds Jamestown, the first permanent English settlement in North America.

1608 After five years of exploring the coast and rivers of North America, Champlain founds Quebec—the first permanent French settlement on the mainland of North America.

1609 Henry Hudson, an English navigator sailing for the Dutch East India Company, explores Chesapeake and Delaware bays, discovers the Hudson River, and claims all the land along its banks for the Netherlands.

1610 Accompanied by 150 new colonists, Lord de la Warr arrives in Jamestown as military governor of Virginia, rescuing the colony from abandonment.
• Spanish settlers under governor Don Pedro de Peralta found Villa Real de la Santa Fe de San Francisco de Asis (now Santa Fe, New Mexico).

1612 John Rolfe establishes what will be the most important cash crop of the southern English colonies by cultivating new varieties of tobacco.

• The Virginia Company sends sixty English settlers to the Bermuda Islands.

1613 English colonists sail north from Virginia to destroy Port Royal and other French settlements in Acadia and Maine, beginning 150 years of armed struggle between the two countries for control of eastern North America.

1614 On his second voyage to America, John Smith explores an area he names New England and maps the coast from Maine to Cape Cod.

1615 Champlain joins the Huron Indians in attacking the Iroquois near Lake Ontario, establishing for New France both an alliance and an enemy that will continue for the rest of the century.
• The first Franciscan friars arrive in Quebec to begin French missionary activity in Canada.

1618 The Thirty Years War begins; originally between Protestants and Catholics in central Europe, the conflict becomes complicated as most of Europe joins in.

A German mercenary soldier in the Thirty Years War

1619 The Dutch East India company founds a trading post at Batavia (now Jakarta) in the East Indies to compete with the Portuguese in the profitable Asian spice trade.
• English architect Inigo Jones begins work on Whitehall Palace, a building which popularizes a European style of architecture in England.

1620 On September 6, a company of forty-six Pilgrims sails from Southampton, England, intending to land in the colony of Virginia.

A seventeenth-century ship

The landing of the Pilgrims

1619 The Virginia House of Burgesses, the first elected legislature in the colonies, meets for the first time.
• A Dutch ship arrives in Jamestown carrying the first Africans to arrive in the colony; they are put to work as indentured servants. Another ship brings women from London as wives for the settlers.

1620 Seeking religious freedom, the Pilgrims head for Virginia on the *Mayflower,* but go off course, land on Cape Cod, and later found a colony at Plymouth, Massachusetts.
• Peregrine White becomes the first child born among the New England colonists.

1621 The Plymouth settlers establish a peace treaty with Massasoit, chief of the local Wampanoag Indians, who help the Pilgrims survive the winter.
• The Dutch West India Company is established to promote trading and colonizing in the New World.

• James I of England grants the Acadian lands already claimed by France to Sir William Alexander for the purpose of founding the colony of Nova Scotia (New Scotland).

1622 One-fourth of the Jamestown colonists, 357 people, die in an attack by the Powhatan Indians, which begins two years of war.

1623 The Council for New England, which succeeded the Plymouth Company, establishes fishing and trading settlements in Portsmouth and Dover, New Hampshire.

Seal of the Virginia Company

• Sir Thomas Warner establishes a settlement on St. Kitts (St. Christopher), the first successful English colony in the West Indies.

1624 On behalf of the Dutch West India Company, Dutch colonists establish fur-trading settlements at Fort Orange (Albany, New York) and New Amsterdam (Manhattan Island).
• James I revokes the Virginia Company's charter and takes control of the settlement, making it a royal colony.

1626 By the end of the summer, the Dutch construct over thirty wooden frame houses on the southern tip of Manhattan.

A TIMELINE OF MAJOR EVENTS

PART II *1600-1649 In Search of New Lands: The Quest for Freedom and Prosperity*

WORLD HISTORY

Gustavus Adolphus

1627 Jahangir, the Emperor Mogul of India, dies; he is succeeded by his son, Shah Jahan, who later builds the Taj Mahal as a memorial to his favorite wife.

1628 In desperate need of money, King Charles II of England calls Parliment (which he dissolved two years before) back into session.

1629 William Laud, a bishop in the Church of England, becomes chancellor of Oxford University; Laud's conservative approach to church reform brings him into conflict with the more radical Puritans.

1630 Gustavus Adolphus, King of Sweden, invades the Holy Roman Empire; he is killed in battle two years later.

1630-1642 Some 16,000 colonists from England emigrate to Massachusetts.

1633 France declares war on Spain.

1634 English explorer Thomas James charts the southern shores of Greenland and Hudson Bay in another unsuccessful search for a sea route to Asia.

1635 A group of European scholars founds the Collegium Romanum to study

COLONIAL HISTORY

1627 A Swedish company receives a charter for that nation's first colony in the New World, although the colony (New Sweden, on the Delaware River) will not be founded for another decade.

1628 Plymouth's Miles Standish breaks up the Merriemount settlement (near present-day Quincy, Massachusetts) and deports its founder, Thomas Morton, who had ridiculed the Pilgrims, sold guns to the Indians, and monopolized the fur trade.
• John Endecott, leading a group of about sixty Puritans fleeing religious persecution in England, founds Salem, Massachusetts, for the New England Company.

1629 The Massachusetts Bay Company receives a royal charter granting the company rights to establish settlements between the Charles and Merrimack rivers, in New England.

Governor John Winthrop

1630 Governor John Winthrop and 900 Puritans found a self-governing settlement at Boston in the name of the Massachusetts Bay Company.

1631 The Council for New England, with Englishman Sir Ferdinando Gorges as president, establishes a single plantation settlement at Saco Bay, Maine.

1632 The English return Quebec and Acadia to French control by a treaty under which each nation recognizes the other's established North American colonies.

1633 Dutch traders from New Amsterdam build a fort and trading post at the juncture of the Connecticut and Park rivers, near present-day Hartford.

1634 Under a charter granted to Cecilius Calvert, the second Lord Baltimore founds Maryland as a refuge for English Catholics who are seeking religious tolerance and civil rights.

The Baltimore arms

1635 Seeking greater freedom than the Massachusetts Bay Colony offered, Thomas Hooker and sixty followers found Hartford, the first permanent settlement in Connecticut.
• English Puritans build the settlement of Fort Saybrook at the mouth of the Connecticut River, beginning competition with the Dutch for control of the river valley.
• French colonists under Pierre Belain, sieur d'Esnambuc, establish a settlement on Martinique and seize the island of Guadaloupe, the first permanent French colony in the West Indies.

1636 Banished from Massachusetts for his religious and political views, Roger Williams founds Providence Plantation (later the colony of Rhode Island), on land he purchases from the Narragansett Indians.

remaining examples of classical art and architecture; the group helps lay the foundation for the modern science of archaeology.

1637 Russian explorers reach the Pacific Ocean. •Teatro San Cassiano, the first public opera house in the world, opens in Venice, Italy. •Ben Jonson, English poet and dramatist, dies.

1639 Through a series of decrees, Japan is closed to foreigners.

1641 Catholics revolt in Ireland and some 30,000 Protestants are massacred.

1642 The English Civil War begins. It is a conflict between supporters of Charles I and the Church of England, and Puritan supporters of Parliament.

1646 Charles I's forces are defeated, ending the English Civil War.

1648 The Peace of Westphalia ends the Thirty Years War. The Dutch and Swedish republics are recognized as independent.

1649 Charles I is tried and executed. Oliver Cromwell, now Lord Protector of England, harshly suppresses Catholic rebellions in Ireland. Many Roman Catholics flee England.

Oliver Cromwell

1637 Colonial forces in Connecticut and Massachusetts, allied with the Mohegan and Narragansett Indians, destroy Pequot Indian villages, kill 500 to 600 Pequots, and scatter or enslave the surviving members of the tribe to avenge the murder of several colonists.

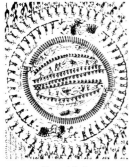

Pequot fort

1638 Banished from Massachusetts for challenging the Puritan clergy, Anne Hutchinson moves to Pocasset (later known as Portsmouth), the second settlement in Rhode Island.

• Puritan clergyman John Davenport, and merchant Theophilus Eaton, who will serve as governor, found the independent Quinnipiac colony at what is now, New Haven, Connecticut.
• Swedish colonists, led by Peter Minuit, establish Fort Christina (Wilmington, Delaware), the oldest permanent settlement in the Delaware River Valley.

Peter Minuit

1639 The Hartford and New Haven colonies establish a democratic, representative system of self-government under the Fundamental Orders of Connecticut.

• The charter for Maine grants the territory already claimed by the French as part of Acadia, to aristocratic English proprietor Sir Ferdinando Gorges.

1641 The colonial government of Massachusetts takes control over the region known as New Hampshire.

1642 Paul de Chomedey, sieur de Maisonneuve, founds the settlement of Montreal, expanding New France's fur trade south and west.

1643 Four New England settlements (Plymouth, Massachusetts Bay, Connecticut, and New Haven) form the United Colonies of New England, joining in defense against both Indians and the Dutch.

1644 Roger Williams returns from England after obtaining a royal patent for the colony of Rhode Island.

1647 Four Rhode Island settlements (Providence, Portsmouth, Newport, and Warwick) join in a loose confederacy, drafting a code of civil law that expressly separates church and state.

Roger Williams

SAMUEL DE CHAMPLAIN

France did not attempt to establish a permanent settlement in Canada until 1604. From 1604 to 1607, Samuel de Champlain accompanied an expedition of French settlers in the New World. He explored the northern Atlantic coast and inland rivers during the summers. During the harsh winter months, however, the French settlers did little more than try to survive.

In 1608, Champlain—now leading the expedition—founded the colony of Quebec. This colony, the capital of New France, became the foundation of France's empire in Canada. On one of the earlier expeditions, the French had joined with the Hurons, who now controlled much of the territory held in the previous century by the Iroquois.

In 1609 and 1610, Champlain and the French settlers helped the Hurons to defeat the Iroquois in several battles, strengthening the ties between them. As a result, the French were able to establish a trading network that stretched all the way to the Huron Indians along the Great Lakes. In the twenty-five years under Champlain's leadership, France won control of both the St. Lawrence River and the fur trade that depended heavily on this river.

Samuel de Champlain (1567-1635; above), noted French geographer and explorer, first explored the New World in 1603 as an "observer" under Captain François Grave du Pont. Upon his return to France, Champlain published Les Sauvages, *an account of his experiences and observations. Champlain accompanied several other expeditions to New France before leading the first colonization effort in 1608. In 1609, he opened up the interior of New France for French fur traders by sailing down the St. Lawrence River and then up to the lake that today bears his name.*

In the search for a site for a permanent settlement, Champlain explored the Atlantic coast and its rivers from 1604 to 1607. In 1605, he sailed south from the St. Croix River that today separates Canada from Maine, and sailed as far south as Cape Cod. In the process, he charted the northern Atlantic coast of North America, producing accurate maps of the area (right) from French Acadia (now Nova Scotia) all the way to Cape Cod.

Champlain favored Quebec as a site for the capital of New France because of its location on the St. Lawrence River. This strategic location allowed France to control traffic on the river—and therefore the northern fur trade. This print of the colony, drawn by Champlain, shows his house (the foremost building), as well as housing for other settlers. Champlain held the colony of Quebec until 1629, when English forces captured the fort. The British returned Quebec to the French three years later.

THE ENGLISH CONTINUE EXPLORATIONS

Although Sir Walter Raleigh's expedition had failed to establish an English colony in the New World, other explorers took up the challenge. In 1602, Bartholomew Gosnold had the first significant success in the New World since the disappearance of the Lost Colony at Roanoke fifteen years earlier. Gosnold navigated the Atlantic coast from Maine to Narragansett Bay, returning to England later that year with a rich cargo of furs, lumber, and sassafras, which was prized in England as a medicinal herb. The Englishmen also brought home turtles and tobacco presented to them by local Indians.

Although Gosnold didn't establish a colony in Massachusetts, he became one of the biggest supporters of North American colonization. When King James I granted the Virginia Company of London a charter in 1606, Gosnold was named vice admiral of the fleet of three ships sent to establish a colony in Virginia. That expedition—led by Gosnold, John Smith, and Christopher Newport— established Jamestown Colony in 1607. Their efforts resulted in the first permanent English colony in America.

Commanded by Bartholomew Gosnold, the Concord *set sail from England on March 26, 1602. Gosnold explored the northern Atlantic coast (opposite, top) from present-day Maine south to Massachusetts, aided by a map of the coast drawn by helpful Native Americans. In the course of his explorations, Gosnold named Cape Cod and several islands in Nantucket Sound and Narragansett Bay—including Martha's Vineyard, which he named after his daughter. Gosnold returned to the New World in 1607 as part of the expedition that founded the Jamestown colony, where he died of malaria later that year.*

Captains John Smith and Christopher Newport (opposite, bottom) joined Gosnold in leading the expedition that founded the first permanent English colony in North America. Financed by the Virginia Company of London, three ships with 105 colonists set sail for Virginia in December 1606. They arrived in Chesapeake Bay in April 1607 and landed thirty miles up the James River on May 14, 1607. The settlers named their colony Jamestown, after King James I.

THE JAMESTOWN SETTLEMENT

Life at Jamestown was a harsh struggle for survival for the English colonists. The settlers at Jamestown endured shortages of food and outbreaks of disease during the first years in Virginia. These hardships were made worse by often tense relations between the colonists and the Virginia Indians and fierce disagreements among the colonists themselves. In September 1608, Captain John Smith became president of the colony. Through a combination of diplomacy and force, Smith managed to secure corn from nearby Indians to feed the colonists during the winter of 1608-1609. The colony grew under Smith, who directed the expansion of the fort, the building of houses, and the planting of crops.

The colony fell into chaos, however, after Smith returned to England in the autumn of 1609. The winter of 1609-10 was so brutal that the colonists called it the "Starving Time." The survivors were abandoning the settlement in 1610 when a relief expedition led by Lord De la Warr, a member of the council of the Virginia Company of London, arrived. De la Warr found the settlement a "very noisome and unwholesome place." He rescued the colony, restoring order through his firm rule. In time, the Jamestown colony became prosperous through tobacco cultivation. Jamestown was also the site of the first representative government in the colonies—and the first English colony in North America to use African slaves.

In his explorations, John Smith managed to establish trade with the Indians. In December 1607, however, on an expedition to trade beads and metal tools for corn, Smith was captured by the powerful Indian leader Powhatan (opposite, top), who reigned over an area of 8,500 square miles. Powhatan apparently planned to put Smith to death. But at the last minute, according to Smith's own account, his life was saved by the chief's young daughter Pocahontas, who (he later wrote) threw herself between Smith and his executioners.

John Smith made several exploring journeys through the territory surrounding Jamestown. He traveled up the rivers of Virginia and drew a remarkably accurate map (opposite, bottom) of the territory. His map, drawn from his own observations as well as from information gained from the Indians, included all existing rivers, islands, and mountains in the region.

Thomas West, Lord De la Warr (1577-1618; left), was named governor of Virginia in 1610. He had the task of saving Jamestown from disaster brought on by hunger, disease, and conflict. With three ships, 150 settlers, and much-needed supplies, Lord De la Warr arrived at Jamestown on June 10, 1610—just in time to prevent the colonists from abandoning the settlement. Ruling the colony strictly, De la Warr constructed two forts at the mouth of the James River, and rebuilt the colony's church and houses. He became sick with typhoid fever and was forced to return to England in 1611.

The Jamestown settlement established the first elected legislature system of government in the colonies, the Virginia House of Burgesses. The first general assembly in the New World met in a small church in August, 1619. Delegates to the House of Burgesses were elected by "freemen" in the colony. The House of Burgesses moved to this building (right) in Williamsburg, Virginia, in 1669.

The English colonists never found the gold they had hoped to find in Virginia, but the Jamestown colony became a commercial success through the cultivation of tobacco. By 1622, the settlers had constructed dozens of houses within the main fortifications (right), several outlying forts, and the first Anglican church in America.

THE PILGRIMS ARRIVE IN THE NEW WORLD

The Pilgrims, also called Separatists for their desire to separate from the established Church of England, became the first permanent settlers in New England. The Pilgrims first went to Holland to escape religious persecution in England. Seeking greater freedom, thirty-five Pilgrims—joined by almost seventy nonseparatists hired by the company that financed the settlement—came to the New World on the *Mayflower* in 1620. The overcrowded *Mayflower* left Plymouth, England, on September 16, 1620, heading for territory its passengers had been granted in Virginia. Bad weather altered the ship's course, however.

Because the colonists would have to land outside the territory granted to them, the Pilgrim leaders realized that some form of self-government would be necessary for their settlement. The result was the Mayflower Compact, which later became the basis for the government of the New Plymouth colony and ensured unity and peace among the colonists. The forty-one men who signed this agreement while still on board the *Mayflower* bound themselves into a civic body and promised to abide by the laws that they would later make. After stopping briefly at Cape Cod in November, the passengers of the *Mayflower* founded the New Plymouth colony in December 1620.

Edward Winslow (1595-1655; above), a passenger on the Mayflower, *served three terms as governor of the Plymouth colony. Winslow's wife died shortly after arriving in the New World, but he married again in May 1621—the first marriage among the New England colonists. Winslow helped the colonists survive by winning the friendship of Massasoit, chief of the local Wampanoag Indians.*

After two months of rough travel on board the Mayflower, *the ship dropped anchor in Plymouth Harbor on December 21, 1620 (opposite, top). A party of sixteen men, led by Captain Miles Standish, went ashore and judged the land suitable for settlement. On the day after Christmas, 102 settlers— many tired, sick, and hungry after the voyage—moved from the ship to the shores of their new colony, which they named New Plymouth.*

The Pilgrims came to America seeking religious freedom. This painting (opposite, bottom) shows them on their way to church, which they attended daily. Their religious conviction sustained the Pilgrims through hard times.

THE PURITANS IN NEW ENGLAND

Another group seeking religious freedom, the Puritans, soon followed the Pilgrims to New England. (The Puritans and Pilgrims held the same basic beliefs, but the Puritans hoped to "purify" the Church of England from within rather than separating from it completely.) During the 1630s, about 20,000 Puritan refugees from England founded Boston, Salem, and the Massachusetts Bay Colony under Governor John Winthrop.

The Puritans established, "Puritan Commonwealth," a government in which only church members had the right to vote. The rigidity of the Puritan government created some disagreements among the settlers, which led to the departure of some settlers and the founding of other New England colonies. In 1636, pastor Roger Williams, banished from Massachusetts for his "dangerous" views regarding religious freedom, founded Providence and the colony of Rhode Island. A year earlier, Reverend Thomas Hooker had left the colony, leading a group of followers seeking religious liberty. Hooker objected to the almost tyrannical control exercised over both religious and civil matters by Reverend John Cotton, head of the First Church of Boston. After Hooker established a settlement at Hartford, Connecticut, his congregation joined him in 1636. Two years later, another wave of English Puritans—headed by John Davenport and Theophilus Eaton—founded New Haven on the Connecticut coast.

This nineteenth century engraving (opposite, top) shows members of Thomas Hooker's church congregation on their way from Massachusetts to Connecticut. In 1635 and 1936, Hooker established three towns along the Connecticut River: Hartford, Wethersfield, and Windsor. Unlike the Dutch traders who came before them, the Puritans led by Hooker intended to found permanent communities, so they brought their families and livestock with them..

This stone house (opposite, bottom) still stands in Guilford, a town on Long Island Sound that was founded a few years after Thomas Hooker's "River Towns" to the north. Wood was a more common building material than stone in early New England, but stone had a great advantage; a stone house had a better chance surviving fire or an attack.

THE DUTCH AND NEW AMSTERDAM

At the beginning of the seventeenth century, the Dutch East India Company, began sponsoring trading and colonizing expeditions to the New World. In 1609, the company sent English navigator Henry Hudson across the Atlantic. Hudson claimed all the territory along the Hudson River for the Dutch. During the next fifteen years, the Dutch established the "province" of New Netherland, which included territory in present-day New York, Long Island, Connecticut, New Jersey, and Delaware. In 1626, a party of Dutch colonists led by Peter Minuit purchased the island of Manhattan from the Canarsee Indians for the equivalent (according to legend) of $24.

The Dutch occupied the Hudson River Valley for over fifty years, and led by Peter Stuyvesant, took control of the small Swedish settlements in the Delaware River valley in 1650.

In 1664, during an English-Dutch war in Europe, a British fleet conquered New Netherland, ending the era of Dutch domination. The victors renamed the city and the surrounding region New York.

The Dutch settlers built high and narrow houses constructed primarily from brick and stone. This row of Dutch houses (below) was built in Albany, which the Dutch called Fort Orange, about 130 miles north of New Amsterdam on the Hudson River.

Henry Hudson, commissioned by the Dutch East India Company to find a northeast passage to the Orient, set sail in the Half Moon *on April 6, 1609. When ice in Arctic waters prevented him from continuing his voyage, he changed course to seek the northwest passage instead. After crossing the Atlantic, Hudson's search led him on September 3, 1609, to the river that today bears his name (right). Hudson sailed 150 miles up the river before he realized that it would not lead to the Pacific. Hudson then claimed all the territory on the east bank (up to present-day Albany) for the Dutch government.*

The Delaware Valley had first been settled in 1638 by mostly Swedish colonists led by the Dutch commander Peter Minuit. The Dutch asserted their claim to the area in 1650, when they forced settlers out of New Sweden. The English captured the Dutch holdings in 1664, but the Dutch government persisted in their claim to the territory, despite the fact that they recovered it only briefly in 1673. This 1666 chart of New Netherland on the Delaware ignores the English conquest of the region two years earlier.

In 1646, Peter Stuyvesant (c. 1592-1672) arrived in New Amsterdam as the director general of all Dutch possessions in North America and the Caribbean. Stuyvesant angered many townspeople with his stern rule. In response to local demands for self-government, he created an advisory council in 1647. In 1650, Stuyvesant forced Swedish colonists from their settlements on the Delaware and made peace with local Indians. In 1664, however, Stuyvesant was forced to surrender New Amsterdam to the British, who renamed it New York.

Under Peter Minuit's command, the Dutch built a fort (below) on the southern tip of Manhattan Island to protect settlers—not from the attacks of local Indians, but from the invasions of other Europeans. The Dutch settlers then constructed houses and attempted to establish farms around the fort. "This island is somewhat less fertile than other spots and gives more trouble on account of the multitude of herbs and trees," wrote Reverend Jonas Michaelius. Turning from farming, the Dutch made the island a center for foreign commerce and trade with the Indians. By 1653, New Amsterdam had over eight hundred residents. This 1651 depiction provides the earliest known view of New Amsterdam.

Part III: 1650-1775
Growth and Expansion

The Gunning Bedford House, in the town of New Castle, Delaware, was probably built prior to 1730 by the son of one of the town's Dutch founders. The Dutch settlement, founded in 1651 and held briefly by the Swedes before being recaptured by the Dutch and called Niew Amstel, was taken in the 1660s by the British, who renamed it New Castle. The house would later be owned by two state governors: Gunning Bedford, governor from 1796 to 1797, and Caleb P. Bennett, governor from 1833-1836.

In the century before the American Revolution, many colonists were motivated to explore and settle new lands by religious concerns. William Penn founded Pennsylvania in 1681 as a refuge where Quakers and other persecuted religious minorities could practice and preach their religious beliefs freely. In 1733, over fifty years later, James Edward Oglethorpe founded Georgia, the last of the original thirteen colonies that participated in the American Revolution, as a haven for persecuted Protestants and the poor. Meanwhile, French and Spanish Jesuit missionaries, hoping to convert Indians to Christianity, did much of the first exploration of what would become the French and Spanish territories in North America. The continuing flow of immigrants helped the colonies grow, especially the English settlements east of the Appalachians.

Despite the original charters that granted ownership of these colonies to commercial interests or sole proprietors, the British crown eventually claimed and took control of all the colonies along the Atlantic coast. The French were exploring the Mississippi Valley and the Gulf coast. The British claimed ownership not only of their original colonies, but of an indefinite expanse of land to the west of these settled lands as well. The Spanish settlements in North America, however, with the notable exception of their Florida colony, were scattered throughout the southwest region of North America, too far away to lead to violent conflicts with other colonists. As the population in the colonies grew through births and immigration, small settlements grew into large cities—Philadelphia, New York, Boston, and New Orleans. Much of the land around these cities was already claimed, so those who preferred farming to trade began to look to the promise of land to the west.

A TIMELINE OF MAJOR EVENTS

PART III *1650-1775 Growth and Expansion*

1652 · 1699

WORLD HISTORY

1662 Margaret Cavendish, Duchess of Newcastle, publishes her *Orations of Diverse Persons,* which maintains that women are the more powerful sex.

1666 London is almost destroyed by the "Great Fire," which begins in a bakery and rages for four days.

1670 In the Treaty of Madrid, Spain recognizes some of England's claim to the West Indies.

1672 William of Orange (later William the III of England) is made Captain-General of the United Provinces (the

The Great Fire of London

Netherlands).
• England's Royal African Company wins exclusive right to capture African slaves for sale in the New World. The monopoly covers the African coast from Morocco to the Cape of Good Hope.

1688 In England's "Glorious Revolution", King James II is overthrown. William of Orange takes his place.

COLONIAL HISTORY

1652 The Massachusetts Bay Colony takes over the territory of Maine and declares itself independent of the English Parliament.

1653 The Dutch West India Company allows New Amsterdam, with over 800 residents, to incorporate as a self-governing city.

1654 Ships carrying Dutch settlers from Brazil, where they had been expelled, bring the first Jews to New Amsterdam.
• In their continuing effort to monopolize the northern fishing and fur trade, English colonists capture Acadia (Nova Scotia) from the French.

1655 Led by Peter Stuyvesant, the Dutch capture Fort Christina and take control of all of the Delaware Valley.

1663 Charles II, King of England, grants

Carolina, portions of which were first settled by Virginia colonists ten years earlier, to eight wealthy proprietors.

1664 The English capture New Amsterdam, which they rename New York, and England's King Charles II grants to his brother, the Duke of York, all land from Maine to Delaware not already settled by English colonists.

1665 The colony of New Jersey, presented by the Duke of York to his friends George Carteret and John Berkeley, is founded.

1668 Jesuit Father Jacques Marquette founds a mission at Sault Ste. Marie in present-day Michigan.

1669 French fur trader Louis Joliet begins his exploration of the Great Lakes region.

1673 Dutch forces

recapture New York and the colonies along the Delaware River from the English, only to be forced to give them back again a year later.
• Joliet and Marquette, hoping to find a river route to the Pacific, explore the Mississippi River as far south as the Arkansas River.

1675 King Philip's War—between English colonists and Native American tribes in Massachusetts, Rhode Island, and Connecticut—causes damage or destruction in sixty-four colonial towns and destroys Indian villages and food supplies.

1682 After almost two years of traveling the Mississippi River, René Robert Cavelier, sieur de La Salle, reaches the river's mouth and claims for France all the land along its banks, a territory he names Louisiana.
• William Penn founds Philadelphia and the

Pennsylvania colony as a refuge for Quakers and other persecuted religious minorities.

1689 Following the "Glorious Revolution" that results in the overthrow of King James II, New England colonies unseat the extremely unpopular royal governor, Edmund Andros, and resume their former separate governments.

1698 Father Eusebio Francisco Kino leads a three-year expedition that charts a land course from Mexico to California, disproving the previous belief that California was an island.

1699 Brothers Pierre and Jean Baptiste Le Moyne establish Old Biloxi (present-day Ocean Springs, Mississippi), the first of several French settlements along the coast of the Gulf of Mexico.

1701 The question of who will rule Spain and its empire leads to the War of the Spanish Succession; eventually, Spain and France are opposed by England, Holland, and several other states.

1713 The Treaty of Utrecht ends the War of the Spanish Succession.

1714 Queen Anne of England dies and is succeeded by the German George I, a great-grandson of James I.

Maria Teresa of Austria

1745 Frederick II, "the Great," becomes king of Prussia.

1745 Charles Edward Stuart, grandson of James II, arrives in Scotland in an attempt to restore Britain to Stuart rule.
• The War of the Austrian Succession begins when Frederick II of Prussia invades Maria Teresa's Austrian province of Silesia. The Treaty of Aix-la-Chapelle ends the war and returns all lands to Austria except Silesia.

Charles Edward Stuart

1700 French settlers begin to construct forts, settlements, fur-trading posts, and Jesuit missions in the Illinois Territory.

1702 Queen Anne's War—the second war between England and France for control of North America—begins. Most of the fighting over the next twelve years will take place in the outlying settlements on the New England-Canada frontier.

1710 British and New England troops capture Port Royal, which they rename Annapolis Royal, and the region of Acadia now known as Nova Scotia, from the French.

1711 Almost 200 North Carolina settlers are massacred by the local Tuscarora Indians, initiating the year-long Tuscarora War, which results in the deaths of hundreds of Tuscaroras and the migration of the survivors to New York, where they join the Iroquois Confederation.

1716 Virginia Governor Alexander Spotswood leads an expedition into the westernmost Virginia territory, crossing the Blue Ridge Mountains into the Shenandoah River Valley.

1718 On behalf of the French Company of the West, Jean Baptiste Le Moyne founds a city (New Orleans) at the mouth of the Mississippi which becomes capital of the Louisiana territory four years later.
• Spanish settlers found the military post and mission of San Antonio, the first of several missions established in an attempt to counter French settlements along the western Gulf coast.

1720 France's treasury is bankrupted after the Mississippi Company is

The Seal of the Mississippi Company

revealed to be a sham in a financially disastrous settlement plan known as the Mississippi Bubble.

1722 The Six Nations of the Iroquois Confederation (Mohawk, Oneida, Onondaga, Cayuga, Seneca, and Tuscarora), under a treaty with Virginia colonists, agree not to cross the Potomac River or move west of the Blue Ridge Mountains.

1729 French soldiers in the Louisiana territory massacre Natchez Indians. A ten-year war begins between the French and Indians.

1733 James Edward Oglethorpe founds the city of Savannah and the colony of Georgia, the last of the original thirteen English colonies, as a haven for the poor.

1747 Settlers from Virginia and Pennsylvania move onto land granted to the Ohio Company, prompting French settlers to construct a line of forts across western Pennsylvania.

1749 Georgia permits large landholdings and slavery, leading to economic prosperity for plantation owners. Following five years of war between French and British colonies (King George's War) in which little territory changes hands, the British found Halifax to strengthen their hold on Nova Scotia.

A TIMELINE OF MAJOR EVENTS

PART III *1650-1775 Growth and Expansion*

WORLD HISTORY

1756 Frederick the Great learns of a secret agreement between six European states (including France and Russia) to divide up Prussia; the Seven Years' War begins with a Prussian attack on Austria. Britain allies itself with Prussia and declares war on France. Britain seizes the island of Minorca in the Mediterranean.
•William Pitt the elder becomes Britain's secretary of state; his vigorous leadership plays a major role in Britain's rise as a world power.

1757 Robert Clive establishes the rule of the British East India Company over most of India.

1760 George III becomes king of Great Britain following the death of his grandfather, George II.
• After years of back-and-forth fighting in Europe, Prussia suffers a series of battlefield defeats. French forces in India are defeated by the British, ending France's hope for a colonial empire in that region.

1761 Catherine II, "the Great," becomes Czarina of Russia.

1763 The Treaty of Paris ends the Seven Years' War, with Britain the clear winner.

1768 In one of a series of important voyages, British Captain James Cook explores and charts the coasts of Australia and New Zealand.

Catherine II

COLONIAL HISTORY

1750 German crafts-people in Pennsylvania develop the Conestoga wagon, soon to become the standard vehicle on the frontier.

1752 A year before their original charter is due to expire, the trustees of Georgia give all administrative power to the British government.

Conestoga wagon

1754 Competing British, French, and Native American claims to territory from the Appalachians west to the Mississippi lead to the nine years of fighting known as the French and Indian War. Meeting in the Albany Convention to discuss the possibility of a treaty with the Iroquois just before the outbreak of the French and Indian War, delegates of seven northern colonies approve Benjamin Franklin's proposal for a union of the colonies.

A cartoon urging unity

The plan is rejected by the colonial legislatures.

1755 Britain banishes defeated French colonists from Acadia, some of whom travel to Louisiana, where they become known as Acadians (Cajuns).

1760 The English capture Montreal from the French, essentially ending the war in America.

1763 Trying to lower the costs of defending frontier settlements from Indian attack, the British government issues a proclamation banning settlement west of the Appalachians.

1764 New Orleans trader Pierre Laclede Liguest founds St. Louis as a fur-trading post.

1767 Britain's Townshend Acts impose more taxes on the colonies.

1769 Father Junípero Serra, a Franciscan monk, and Don Gaspar de Portolá, the governor

Father Serra

of Lower California, found the first California missions in San Diego and Monterey, establishing Spanish control of the Pacific Coast from San Francisco Bay to South America.

1770 Lord Frederick North becomes prime minister of Britain; he is determined to assert British control over the American colonies.

1772 Poland, formerly an independent nation, is divided among Russia, Austria, and Prussia.

1773 Parliament passes the Regulating Act, placing many functions of the British East India Company under control of the government.

1773 Pope Clement XIV dissolves the Jesuit Order.

1774 Louis XVI becomes king of France.
•Parliament passes the Coercive Acts in an attempt to crush growing colonial resistance to British rule. The Acts close the port of Boston and reduce the power of the Massachusetts legislature.

1775 Scottish inventor Isaac Watt develops an improved steam engine; his invention encourages the growing Industrial Revolution in Britain.

1775 Lord North extends the New England Restraining Act to South Carolina, Virginia, Pennsylvania, Maryland, and New Jersey. The act forbids trade with any country other than Britain and Ireland.

Edmund Burke

1770 Christopher Dock publishes the *Schul-Ordnung* to promote public education among German immigrants in Pennsylvania.

Thomas Jefferson

• Thomas Jefferson urges the Virginia Legislature to pass a law establishing freedom of religion in that colony.
• Virginia's Indian commissioner negotiates a treaty with Cherokee Indians that extends that colony's land by some 9,000 square miles.

1771 The New Hampshire colony is divided into five counties in order to better govern the large increase in settlement. The town meeting remains the main form of governing.

1772 Spanish explorers led by Captain Pedro Fages penetrate the San Joaquin and Sacramento valleys in present-day California.

1773 John Sevier of Virginia and James Robertson of North Carolina found the Watauga Association to govern the area ceded to Britain by the Six Nations of the Iroquois (east Tennessee); this is the first local independent government in the American colonies.

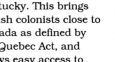

A French colonial cottage on the western frontier

• Spanish colonial authorities establish a formal government for their new settlements in California.

1774 James Harrod leads a party of Pennsylvania traders up the Kentucky River to found Harrodsburg, at the head of the Salt River (the first European settlement in Kentucky).

Daniel Boone rescuing his daughter Jemina

1775 In Sycamore Shoals, Kentucky, the Transylvania Land Company gains a treaty with the Cherokees, for all land between the Ohio and Cumberland rivers, and west of Appalachian Mountains, in exchange for $10,000 in goods.
• Daniel Boone helps build the Wilderness Road through the Cumberland Gap of the Appalachian Mountains and establishes Boonesborough in Kentucky. This brings British colonists close to Canada as defined by the Quebec Act, and allows easy access to Ohio, Illinois, and Indiana territory.

TERRITORIES AND LAND CLAIMS

In the second half of the seventeenth century, English colonists claimed and settled more and more territory in the New World. William Penn, a Quaker who had been imprisoned four times for publicly stating and printing his religious beliefs in England, gained a grant of land in North America from England's King Charles II in payment for a debt the crown owed Penn's father. In 1681, the king signed a charter naming Penn sole owner and supreme governor of the colony of Pennsylvania. The next year, Penn founded the colony as a refuge for Quakers and others persecuted for their religious beliefs. Penn's colony, noted for its fair treatment of the local Indians, formally purchased the land from three Delaware chiefs in 1683.

Penn believed in both religious tolerance and self-government. He spent most of the next fifteen years in England defending the right of the colonies to exist independently, a right that the English crown seemed intent on undermining.

The English had by this time established themselves as the dominant colonial power on the Atlantic coast of North America. Indeed, the established colonies had become so bold that they sometimes claimed ownership of much more territory than they had settled. These land claims led, in the eighteenth century, to the planning and settling of towns and cities and to further westward expansion.

Penn had sent agents to settle his colony almost a year before he was able to visit in 1682. These settlers had begun building a city residence, parts of which were prepared in England, for Penn even before he arrived. Penn lived in the city for only two years before returning to England to defend the self-rule of his colony, a fight that would keep him away from Pennsylvania for the next fifteen years. A portion of Penn's house (above) still stands on the west side of Letitia Street in Philadelphia.

Philadelphia, the foremost city in the Pennsylvania colony, was founded in 1681 by William Penn. This 1698 map (opposite, bottom) shows some of the lots divided among the town founders—most notably Penn and his daughter, Letitia. Though Penn was still in England, defending the interests of his colony, he had sent instructions to town planners expressing his desire for every house to be situated in the middle of its own plot, to ensure "that it may be a greene Country Towne." By the time Penn returned for his second visit in 1699, the city population had grown to ten thousand.

This map (right) shows all English colonial grants and actual settlements in the New World during the seventeenth century. Note that many colonial grants claimed not only a specific tract of land, but also "indefinite westward extension." The land "claimed" by Massachusetts and Connecticut stretches westward far beyond the area actually settled by 1700. This vague land claim would become the basis for westward expansion in North America, spurring further exploration and settlement.

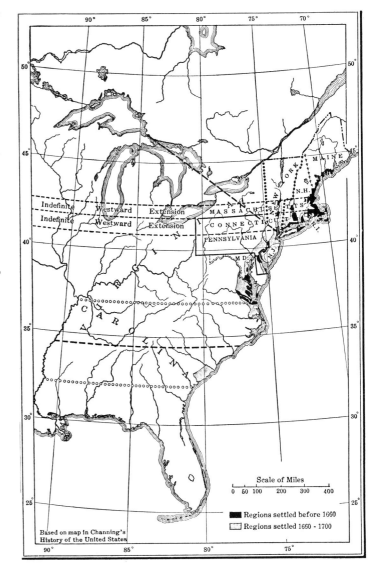

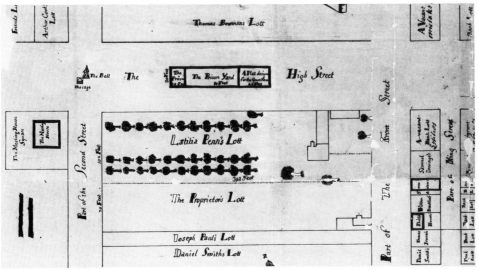

THE SPANISH
IN CALIFORNIA

Beginning in the 1720s, Russian adventurers began exploring and settling the Pacific northwest of America. When Spanish settlers heard that the Russians had started to move south from present-day Alaska, they decided to take measures to prevent Russian land gains in territory they considered part of New Spain. To accomplish this end, the Viceroy (Governor) of New Spain organized an expedition of colonists and Jesuit missionaries to move northward from present-day Mexico and Baja (Lower) California.

The expedition to convert the Indians of Upper California to Roman Catholicism and establish claims to the land was led by Don Gaspar de Portolá, the governor of Lower California, and Father Junípero Serra, a Franciscan monk. After founding the first California mission in San Diego on July 16, 1769, Portolá, Serra, and forty others marched northward all the way to Monterey, just south of present-day San Francisco. Serra ultimately established nine California missions from San Francisco to San Diego. Serra, a staunch defender of the local Indians, helped introduce cattle, sheep, grains, and the fruits of Mexico to Upper California. The work of Serra and the other Jesuit missionaries played a critical role in securing and strengthening Spain's control of the area.

-:(✠):-

ESTRACTO DE NOTICIAS

del Puerto de Monterrey, *de la Mission, y Presidio que se han establecido en el con la denominacion de* San Carlos, *y del sucesso de las dos Expediciones de Mar, y Tierra que à este fin se despacharon en el año proximo anterior de* 1769.

DESPUES DE LAS REPETIDAS, y costosas Expediciones que se hicieron por la Corona de España en los dos siglos antecedentes para el reconocimiento de la Costa Occidental de Californias, por la mar del Sur, y la ocupacion del importante Puerto de Monterrey, se ha logrado ahora felizmente esta empressa con las dos Expedicionos de mar, y tierra que à consequencia de Real Orden, y por disposicion de este Superior Govierno, se despacharon desde el Cabo de San Lucas, y el Presidio de Loreto en los meses de Enero, Febrero, y Marzo del año proximo anterior.

En Junio de èl se juntaron ambas Expediciones en el Puerto de San Diego, situado à los 32. grados, y medio de latitud, y tomada la resolucion
de

This 1769 notice (above) announces the founding of Monterey, the first Spanish military post in present-day California. The notice, published by order of the Viceroy of New Spain, is the earliest known report on the territory known as Upper California. Monterey, named capital of Alta (Upper) California in 1775, was fortified and made a main port of entry for New Spain. This allowed the Spanish settlers to establish control of the Pacific coast of America from San Francisco Bay south to South America.

Though Spanish explorers had discovered that Baja California was not an island as early as 1539, seventeenth-century maps of the area, drawn mostly by Dutch mapmakers, continued to depict the Gulf of California as a sea that separated Mexico and California. In 1700, however, Father Eusebio Francisco Kino, a Jesuit missionary, discovered and charted a land passage from Mexico to California through present-day Arizona. This map (opposite, top) shows the course followed by Father Kino from 1698 to 1701.

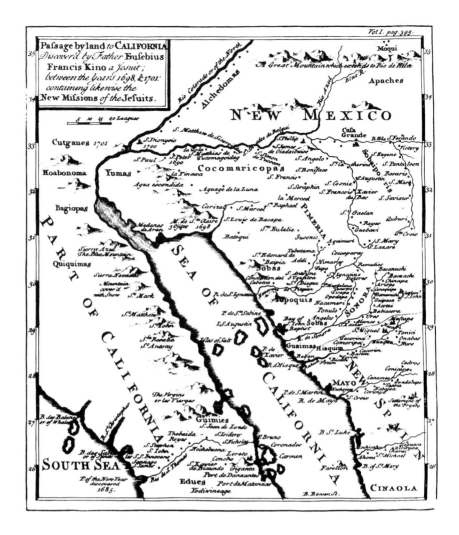

Monterey Bay was first explored by Europeans in 1602 by Sebastian Vizcaino, who named the area after the viceroy of Mexico, the Count of Monte Rey. In 1770, over 150 years later, Father Junípero Serra founded his second California mission there. Father Serra, who went on to found seven more California missions, was buried in the mission's sanctuary in 1784.

FRENCH EXPLORATIONS IN THE GREAT LAKES

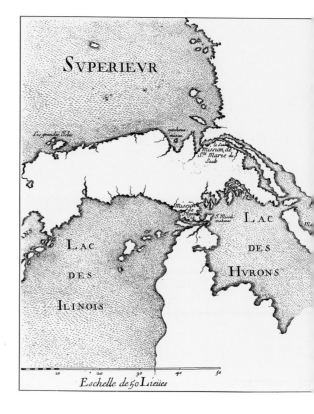

The French began expeditions to expand their territorial holdings and influence in the New World in the 1660s. They were motivated by two very different incentives: the fur trade and the church. In the 1660s and 1670s, these French adventurers began moving westward from Quebec, the capital of New France, into the Great Lakes region.

Fur trader and adventurer Louis Joliet explored the Great Lakes and the surrounding territory from 1669 to 1672. Commissioned by the governor of New France to find a river route to the Pacific in 1674, Joliet and Jesuit priest Jacques Marquette explored the Mississippi River Basin. They canoed as far south as the Arkansas River and discovered from friendly Quapaw Indians that the Mississippi flowed into the Gulf of Mexico rather than the Pacific.

Another French explorer, René Robert Cavelier, sieur de La Salle, explored the territory around the Great Lakes during the 1670s, often accompanied by Father Louis Hennepin, a Franciscan friar who became La Salle's chaplain in 1678. With the support of both King Louis XIV of France and Comte de Frontenac, the governor of New France, La Salle pushed southward down the Mississippi from the Great Lakes territories. The French hoped to confine British settlements to the Atlantic coast, cutting off the "indefinite westward extension" claimed by English colonies.

This map, first published in 1672, is thought to be the work of Jesuit missionaries Jacques Marquette and Claude Jean Allouez, who explored the Great Lakes regions in the 1660s and 1670s. Father Marquette founded missions at Sault Ste. Marie in 1668 and at St. Ignace (Michilimackinac) in 1671, both in present-day Michigan and both included in the section of the map pictured here (above).

After establishing Fort Crèvecoeur near modern-day Peoria, Illinois, in 1680, La Salle returned to Canada, while his chaplain, Father Louis Hennepin, remained to explore the upper Mississippi River. Captured by Sioux Indians in April 1680, Hennepin accompanied the Indians on hunting expeditions. In this drawing (above), the Sioux are quarreling over the division of the party's goods and equipment. Hennepin was rescued from the Sioux in July by French adventurer Daniel Greysolon, sieur Dulhut, for whom Duluth, Minnesota, is named.

Father Hennepin wrote the first published description of the Great Lakes regions that would later become the Canadian province of Ontario and the states of Michigan, Wisconsin, and Illinois. Illustrations of exotic scenes and creatures such as the buffalo (below), a beast unfamiliar to most Europeans, helped make Hennepin's books extremely popular in the 1680s and 1690s.

René Robert Cavelier (left), sieur de La Salle (1643-1687), arrived in Canada in 1666 and made a fortune as a farmer and fur trader in Montreal. His westward explorations began in the Great Lakes region in 1669. Nine years later, Seneca Indians near Niagara Falls taught La Salle how to survive in the wilderness on game and dried corn. Using these skills, La Salle became the first European to explore the length of the Mississippi River, in a 1681-1682 expedition.

Nine years after Joliet and Marquette traveled down the Mississippi, La Salle descended the river all the way to the Gulf of Mexico. On April 9, 1682, after reaching the mouth of the river by canoe, La Salle claimed the entire region through which the Mississippi flowed for France. He named this territory Louisiana, after King Louis XIV of France. This map (below), drawn in 1684 by Jean Baptiste Louis Franqueli, shows the Indian tribes along the lower Mississippi visited by La Salle.

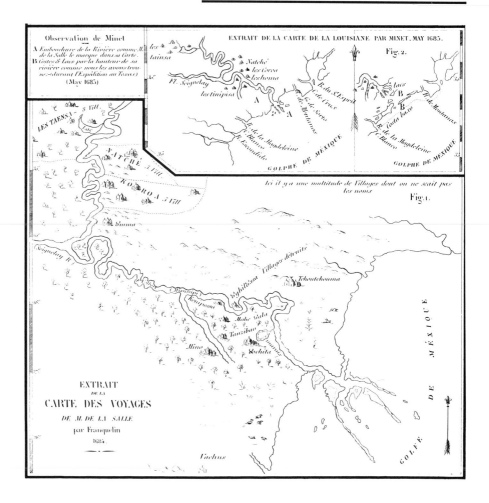

In 1684, La Salle set out from France in an attempt to found a colony on the lower Mississippi. He hoped to use this settlement as a base from which to conquer—or at least harass—Spanish holdings in northern Mexico. The expedition, marked by quarrels between La Salle and the French naval commander, seemed doomed from the start. Many ships fell victim to shipwreck and pirates in the Atlantic, and many of those aboard died of disease. Poor navigation led the surviving ships to land on the coast of Texas, five hundred miles off course. The colonists tried several times to find the mouth of Mississippi from the Gulf of Mexico but could never find it. In March 1687, mutineers took control of the expedition and murdered La Salle.

THE FRENCH LAY CLAIMS ALONG THE GULF COAST

In 1699, fifteen years after La Salle set out on his failed attempt to establish a French colony along the Gulf coast, French colonists began settling in Louisiana. The leaders of the enterprise were two Canadian soldiers and explorers: Pierre Le Moyne, sieur d'Iberville, and his brother Jean Baptiste Le Moyne, sieur de Bienville. In 1699, Iberville, Bienville, and two hundred colonists founded the settlement of Old Biloxi, at the present site of Ocean Springs, Mississippi. This fort served as capital of the Louisiana Territory for the next three years.

In 1701, Iberville was recalled to military service, and Bienville—sixteen years younger than his brother—was named governor of Louisiana. Under his leadership over the next eleven years, further settlements were established, including Fort Louis at the site of present-day Mobile, Alabama. During his second term as governor, which began in 1718, Bienville founded the city of New Orleans at the request of the French Company of the West, which had secured all colonizing rights in the territory. When the Company collapsed several years later, Bienville was forced out of office.

By 1733, when Bienville began his third term as governor, Louisiana had a population of eight thousand. This foundation allowed France to develop this wealthy and strategic area before England or Spain could establish any presence there.

Pierre Le Moyne, sieur d'Iberville (1661-1706), soldier and explorer, was born in Montreal. In 1686, Iberville led a French expedition against English forts on Hudson Bay in Canada. He defended French settlements in Canada from English invaders for the next decade. Although war with Great Britain prevented Iberville from realizing his plan to expand the Louisiana colonies, his efforts had helped France gain a foothold on the Gulf of Mexico.

This map (opposite, top) shows the forts, settlements, rivers, and mountains in the Louisiana Territory (today Louisiana, Mississippi, and Alabama) by the middle of the eighteenth century. The map was drawn by Dumont de Montigny, for his "Histoire de la Louisiane," published around 1740. The map also includes small Indian villages, as well as the general locations (center of the map) of the two largest tribes in the territory: the Choctaw (des Chactas sauvages), who allied themselves with the French, and the Chickasaw (des Chicachas sauvages), who fought several wars against the French settlers.

The city of New Orleans was founded at the mouth of the Mississippi in 1718 by Iberville's brother, Jean Baptiste Le Moyne, sieur de Bienville. The first plan for the city (opposite, bottom) was drafted several years later by Adrien de Pauger, an engineer. This plan shows the area now known as the city's famous Vieux Carrè, or "French Quarter."

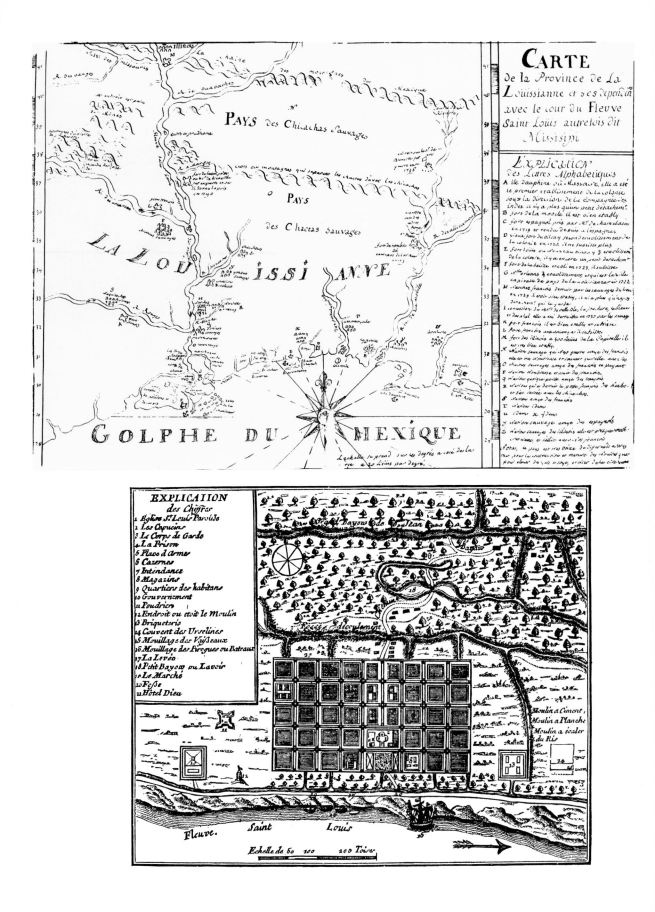

THE MISSISSIPPI BUBBLE LAND EXPLORATION

The French Compagnie d'Occident (Company of the West), established by John Law in 1717, obtained the exclusive right to develop French territories along the Mississippi River and the coast of the Gulf of Mexico. Law's company also quickly gained a monopoly on both the French tobacco and African slave trades. In an ambitious plan to develop the Louisiana territory, the Company—known after 1719 as the Compagnie des Indes (Company of the Indies)—began recruiting German and Dutch settlers to come over and farm the land in exchange for a promise of their own property and supplies. Law's plan, which worked well for several years, allowed the company to gain a monopoly over France's colonial trade.

The enormous profit potential of the company's Mississipi Bubble program, however, led to a buying frenzy that drove the price of shares in the company up by thirty times their original value—well beyond the company's actual earnings potential. When colonial profits came much slower than anticipated, the stock's value plummeted, starting a stock market crash in France. The plan brought financial ruin to most of its investors, promoters, and sponsors. The Company did found the city of New Orleans, however, and brought thousands of settlers to New Biloxi, Natchez, and other settlements in the Louisiana territory.

The coat of arms of the Company of the West (above), also known as the Mississippi Company, figured prominently on promotional pamphlets and brochures used to recruit Dutch and German settlers for the Mississippi Bubble program from 1718 to 1721.

The promotional pamphlets used to foster interest in the Mississippi Bubble program often featured maps (opposite, bottom) of the available territory. This 1720 map, which depicts the French settlement at Fort Biloxi, appeared in Dutch brochures published in 1720 and 1721.

John Law (1671-1729), a Scottish adventurer and financial wizard, originated the Mississippi Bubble scheme to develop the French territories on the Gulf Coast. Law combined his Paris bank (the Banque Generale) with the Compagnie des Indes, a publicly owned company, in order to finance the scheme. Though Law himself wasn't directly responsible for the stock market crash that led to the fall of the Mississippi program, he provided an easy target for blame. Forced to flee France in December 1720, Law died in Venice nine years later. This satiric depiction of Law by a Dutch artist first appeared in a 1720 book on financial schemers called The Great Mirror of Folly.

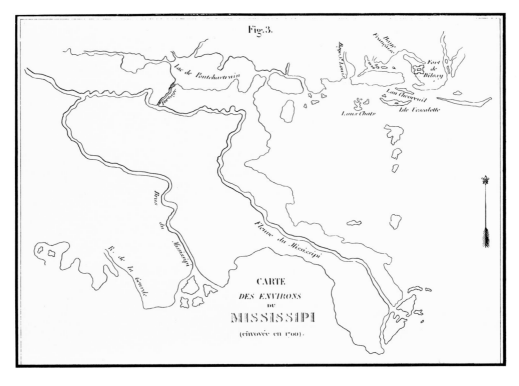

VIRGINIA EXPANDS TO THE WEST

By the eighteenth century, Virginia had over twenty settled counties, consisting mostly of country farms and a few villages formed by the clustering of houses around county courthouses. Virginia considered its frontier counties, populated with scattered pioneers living in the wilderness, to extend westward indefinitely. But the English had neither settled nor explored much territory west of the Appalachians.

Virginia Governor Alexander Spotswood recognized the potential of this unknown territory to support the growing population of his colony. Spurred by the rising birth rate in the colony and the arrival of ever more colonists from England, Spotswood set his sights on the western frontier. Governor Spotswood set out in August 1716 with an expedition into the mountainous wilderness to promote the cause of westward expansion of his territory. Spotswood's expedition journeyed over two hundred miles inland to a mountain range they called the Blue Ridge, because a trick of light had made the mountains appear blue. From these mountains, the party traveled into the Shenandoah River Valley, which lies between the Blue Ridge and the Appalachians. By 1730, Virginia settlers had established settlements, farms, and towns in the Shenandoah Valley. Within ten years, the Virginians had moved beyond the Appalachians into the Ohio country, renewing conflict between English and French settlers.

Alexander Spotswood (1676-1740; above), was named governor in 1710. In organizing and leading the expedition to the Shenandoah Valley in 1716, Spotswood was one of the first British colonial governors to recognize the rich potential of the western frontier.

Virginia's commercial success was based mainly on plantation farming. Plantations (below) were large cultivated estates that depended on labor by white indentured servants and black slaves to plant and harvest crops.

Spotswood drew the young, adventurous horsemen of his expedition mostly from the colonial gentry. Upon their successful return, Spotswood presented each member of the company with a miniature golden horseshoe to commemorate the expedition (below). (Horses, which generally went unshod on the gentle roads of settled Virginia villages, needed shoes to travel the rocky mountains on their westward journey.) For this reason, the members of the expedition were thereafter known as the "Knights of the Golden Horseshoe."

OGLETHORPE AND THE SETTLEMENT OF GEORGIA

Georgia, the last of the original thirteen American colonies to be settled by European colonists, was founded in 1733. In 1732, King George II of Great Britain granted a charter to settle the territory to James Edward Oglethorpe—a soldier, member of Parliament, and philanthropist. Oglethorpe hoped to establish a colony that would offer a fresh start for convicts, debtors, and other poor people, as well as providing a refuge for European Protestants suffering from religious persecution. The British government granted the charter with the intention of using Georgia as a buffer against Spanish colonists to the south and French colonists to the west.

In 1733, Oglethorpe arrived in Charleston, South Carolina with a number of settlers, some paying their own way and others having their expenses paid by the colony's trustees. Oglethorpe called the territory Georgia, in honor of the king.

The outbreak of war between England and Spain in 1739 affected both Georgia and its neighboring Spanish territory, Florida. Georgia did not begin to flourish economically until 1749, when the colony first permitted slavery and large plantations. Three years later, however, the trustees surrendered all power over the colony to the British crown.

In the 1730s and 1740s, many German, Austrian, and Swiss Protestants came to North America to escape religious persecution in Europe. Many German-speaking Lutherans settled in Pennsylvania, as well as the Carolinas and New York. Some accompanied James Oglethorpe among the first settlers of Georgia. Most arrived poor; some had been exiled for speaking out against the lack of religious freedom at home. This engraving (opposite, top) shows Lutherans banished from Salzburg, Austria. Carrying their clothing, copies of the Lutheran Augsburg Confession, and the Bible, these exiled Salzburgers came from Austria to the new colony of Georgia.

Oglethorpe found a site for the first Georgia settlement on the Savannah River. The settlers began building what would become the town of Savannah, which they named after the river. This engraving (opposite, bottom) depicts the construction of Savannah as of March 29, 1734. The city, the birthplace of the Georgia colony, was planned around a system of public squares that would later become small parks. Savannah, which opened its port to trade in 1744, would function as the seat of Georgia's colonial government and, after the American Revolution, as the state capital until 1786.

FROM SETTLEMENTS INTO TOWNS

The growth and increasing prosperity of the colonies had two very different effects on settlement patterns in the eighteenth century. First, once-small settlements, especially those founded on the rivers that emptied into the Atlantic, were transformed into thriving cities. Second, pioneers began moving into previously unsettled lands to the west of these original settlements. The established settlements grew through the continued arrival of more people in the colonies as well as a rising birth rate among earlier settlers. Communities grew first into organized villages, then expanded into towns, and finally cities.

By the middle of the eighteenth century, the three largest cities in the colonies were Philadelphia, New York, and Boston. Despite similarities, each city retained the character of its earliest settlers. The original nationality of each region's settlers was reflected in the different types of residences that each group constructed. The Dutch, Swedish, German, and English settlers all left their mark on Philadelphia and the Delaware Valley settlements. The influence of both the original Dutch settlers and their British conquerors could be seen in New York and the Hudson River Valley. And Boston retained the flavor of its British Puritan settlers.

This house is typical of French dwellings in Illinois prior to 1763, when the British took control of the region. The split-sloped roof and the wide, raised porch that encircled the house were characteristic features of French-American houses of the era.

The Old Dutch House at New Castle, Delaware, which still stands today as a colonial museum, is one of the most notable landmarks from the period of Dutch settlement. Although the origin of the building is unknown, most local historians believe it to have been built in the late 1600s.

This engraving of Boston (above) in the 1760s shows how the city, founded over 130 years earlier by Puritans of the Massachusetts Bay Company, thrived as a seaport. Many New Englanders depended on the sea to provide them with a livelihood: as ship-builders, sailors, fishers, and merchants. The ideal location of Boston, perfect for a seaport, helped it remain one of the largest cities in the British American colonies.

By the 1760s, New York (below) had grown to become second only to Philadelphia among American centers of commerce and foreign trade. Under British control for almost a hundred years, the city had grown into a flourishing business and trade center.

THE WAY WEST

The successful expedition of Alexander Spotswood, combined with the "indefinite westward extension" claimed by the British colonies in America, helped fuel the other important settlement pattern of the mid-eighteenth century: westward expansion. While many new arrivals were content to stay in the already established cities and smaller communities along the Atlantic coast and coastal rivers, others yearned to travel west. The urge to expand westward grew in the years prior to the American Revolution, leading more and more exploring parties to venture into new territory. British settlement on the frontier began slowly: Those few who crossed the Appalachians before the Revolution settled mostly in what would become Kentucky and Tennessee, while the land north of the Ohio River remained largely unsettled until after the war.

Both the Native Americans and the French settlers in the Mississippi Valley increasingly resisted the British colonies' westward movement. This ultimately led to the French and Indian War (1754-1763). Although the French would give up almost all their territory in North America at the end of the war, the conflict inflicted heavy costs on the victorious British. In an attempt to lower the cost of managing their expanded colonial empire, the British government banned settlement west of the Appalachians in 1763. This order from abroad annoyed those pioneers and speculators who, like George Washington, wanted to invest in western ventures.

Among those attracted by the economic promise of westward expansion was Virginia plantation owner, soldier, and future Revolutionary leader George Washington. Washington was interested in a number of business ventures in the West, including those of the Ohio Company and the Mississippi Company. This, the last page of a three-page letter (below) in Washington's hand, was written on June 3, 1763, just four months after the end of the French and Indian War. It outlines the articles of agreement of the Mississippi Land Company, which hoped to acquire 2.5 million acres east of the Mississippi River and north of the Ohio River. The thirty-eight signers of the agreement included Washington, his brother John Augustine, Thomas Lightfoot Lee, and Richard Henry Lee.

The Conestoga wagon (above) was invented by German craftsmen in the Conestoga Creek region of Lancaster County, Pennsylvania, in the mid-eighteenth century. It played an important part in the westward expansion of North American settlements. The Conestoga wagon, pulled by four to six horses or oxen, allowed settlers to haul up to six tons of freight over bad, rocky roads.

Daniel Boone (c.1734-1820), hunter, trapper, and frontier adventurer, helped build the Wilderness Road from eastern Virginia through the Cumberland Gap of the Appalachian Mountains in 1775. This romantic depiction (below) shows Boone rescuing his daughter, Jemina, and Betsey and Frances (Fanny) Calloway, who had been carried off by the Indians while crossing the river opposite Boonesborough in 1776.

Resource Guide

Key to picture positions: (T) top, (C) center, (B) bottom; and in combinations: (TL) top left, (TC) top center, (TR) top right, (BL) bottom left, (BC) bottom center, (BR) bottom right, (CR) center right, (CL) center left.

Key to picture locations within the Library of Congress collections (and where available,

photo-negative numbers): P - Prints and Photographs; HABS - Historical American Buildings Survey (div. of Prints and Photographs); R - Rare Book Division; G - General Collections; MSS - Manuscript Division; G&M - Geography and Map Division.

PICTURES IN THIS VOLUME

2-3 Savannah, P, USZ62-37882 6-7 Oglethorpe, P, USZ62-1922 8-9 map, G 10-11 ships, R

Timeline I:
12 TL, Columbus, G; TR, Charles I, G; BL, map, G; BR, Cortes, G 13 T, Magellan, G; BL, Cartier, P, USZ62-9097; BR, de Soto, P, USZ62-674 14 T, Loyola, G; BL, expedition, P, USZ62-37993; BR, Quebec, G&M 15 T, Drake, G; B, chief, R 16-17 T, mound, G; B, ruins, P, USZ62-46901 18-19 T, Ferdinand, R; B, map, G&M 20-21 TL, shipbuilders, R; BL, jackstaff, R; TR, Columbus, R 22-23 TL, landing, P, USZ62-43535; TR, trading, R; BR, canoe, R 24-25 BL, baking, R; TR, camp, R; BR, cannibals, R 26-27 TL, Vespucci, R; TR, allegory, P; BR, Ponce de León, P 28-29 TL, de Soto, P, USZ62-674; TR, map, G&M 30-31 C, palace, HABS; TR, Coronado, P, USZ62-37993 32-33 TL, Cartier, P, USZ62-9097; TR, ship, R; BR, map, G&M 34-35 TR, Florida, P, USZ62-380; BR, Ft. Caroline, R 36-37 TL, village, R; TR, planting, R; BR, alligator, P, USZ62-373 38-39 TR, Drake, P, USZ62-50791; BR, St. Augustine, R 40-41 TL, Raleigh, P; TR, title page, R; BR, English, P, USZ62-53337 42-43 TL, Secota, R; BR, Indians, R 44-45 TL, fishing, R; TR, pyre, R 46-47 Smith, P, USZ62-10751

Timeline II:
48 T, Elizabeth, G; B, Smith, P, USZ62-10751 49 TL, soldier, G; TR, ship, G; BL, Pilgrims, P; BR, Seal, G 50 T, Gustavus, G; BL, Winthrop, P, USZ62-1007; BR, Arms, G 51 T, Cromwell, G; BL, fort, P, USZ62-37055; BC, Minuit, P, USZ62-33018; BR, Williams, G 52-53 TL, Champlain, P; TR, Quebec, R; BR, map, G&M 54-55 TR, Gosnold, P, USZ62-40631A; BR, Smith, P, USZ62-49745 56-57 TR, Pocahontas, P, USZ62-31735; BR, map, G&M 58-59 TL, De la Warr, P, USZ62-10276; C, Jamestown, G; TR, Burgesses, G 60-61 TL, Winslow, R; TR, Pilgrims, P; BR, church, P, USZ62-3291 62-63 TR, Puritans, P, USZ62-38659; BR, house, P 64-65 BL, houses, P, USZ62-31154; TR,

ship, P, USZ62-43066 66-67 TL, map, P, USZ62-2142; TR, Stuyvesant, P, USZ62-1837; BR, New Amsterdam, P, USZ62-17525 68-69 House, P, USZ62-5150

Timeline III:
70 fire, G; 71 G; TL, Maria Teresa, G; TR, Charles, G; B, Seal, P, USZ62-676 72 T, Catherine, G; BR, wagon, P, USZ62-12695; BC, cartoon, P, USZ62-33765; BR, Serra, G 73 T, Burke, G; BL, Jefferson, G; BC, cottage, P, USZ62-33765; BR, Boone, P, USZ62-1431 74-75 BL, cottage, G; TR, map, G; BR, plan, G 76-77 BL, notice, MSS; TR, map, G&M; BR, mission, P, USZ62-8109 78-79 TL, map, P, USZ62-9286; BL, boats, P, USZ62-2974; TR, Hennepin, R; BR, buffalo, P, USZ62-8171 80-81 TL, La Salle, P, USZ62-5545; BL, map, G&M; TR, death, P, USZ62-5546 82-83 TL, D'Iberville, R; TR, map, MSS; BR, plan, G&M 84-85 TL, Seal, P, USZ62-676; TR, Law, P, USZ62-30700; BR, map, G&M 86-87 TL, Spotswood, R; BL, plantation, HABS; BR, Knights, G 88-89 TR, Salzburgers, P, USZ62-1926; BR, plan, P, USZ62-1912 90-91 TL, French house, P, USZ62-33762; BL, Dutch house, P, USZ62-5153; TR, Boston, P, USZ62-31211; BR, New York, P, USZ62-19360 92-93 BL, letter, MSS; TR, wagon, P, USZ62-12695; BR, Boone, P, USZ62-51136

SUGGESTED READING

Sмith, Carter. *The Jamestown Colony.* New York: Silver Burdett, 1991.
Berger, Josef. *Discoverers of the New World.* Mahwah, NJ: Troll Associates, 1960.
Zinger, Feenie. *The Pilgrims and Plymouth Colony.* Mahwah, NJ: Troll Associates, 1961.
Daniel, Clifton. *Chronicle of America.* New York: Prentice-Hall, 1989.

Morrison, Samuel E. *The Oxford History of the American People.* New York: 1965.
Encyclopedia Brittanica. *The Annals of America,* volume 1. Chicago: Encyclopedia Brittanica, Inc. 1976.
The American Heritage Illustrated History of the United States, volume 1. New York: American Heritage, 1988.
The Life History of the United States, volume 1. Alexandria, Virginia, 1977.

Index

Page numbers in *italics* indicate illustrations.